FROM FRAZZLED TO
FOCUSED

THE ULTIMATE GUIDE
for MOMS WHO WANT to
RECLAIM THEIR TIME,
THEIR SANITY and THEIR LIVES

RIVKA CAROLINE

with *Amy Sweeting*

Illustrations by Liana Finck

RIVER GROVE
BOOKS

Published by River Grove Books
Austin, TX
www.greenleafbookgroup.com

Distributed by River Grove Books

For ordering information or special discounts for bulk purchases, please contact River Grove Books at PO Box 91869, Austin, TX, 78709, 512.891.6100.

Design and composition by Greenleaf Book Group LLC
Cover design by Greenleaf Book Group LLC
Cover image: ©Elnur, 2012. Used under license from Shutterstock.com.
Illustrations by Liana Finck

Publisher's Cataloging-In-Publication Data
(Prepared by The Donohue Group, Inc.)
Caroline, Rivka.
    From frazzled to focused : the ultimate guide for moms who want to reclaim their time, their sanity and their lives / Rivka Caroline with Amy Sweeting ; illustrations by Liana Finck.—1st ed.
        p. : ill. ; cm.
    Issued also as an ebook.
    ISBN: 978-1-938416-25-5
    1. Mothers—Time management. 2. Organization. 3. Orderliness. 4. Stress management for women. I. Sweeting, Amy. II. Finck, Liana. III. Title.
HQ759 .C37 2013
306.874/3   2013933146

Print ISBN: 978-1-938416-25-5
eBook ISBN: 978-1-938416-26-2

First Edition

For my children.
There will be times when you will feel frazzled
and other times
when you will be focused.
Regardless, please make sure to be a mensch
to yourself and others.

Avremel

Menachem

Yossi

Sara

Yaakov

Chana

Rosa

You inspire me daily to be a better person.
I love each of you more than chocolate.

—R.C.

To Rory and Sophie,
for frazzling me in the best of all possible ways,
and to Jamie,
for always keeping me focused.

—A.S.

CONTENTS

PART II: THE SYSTEM IS THE SOLUTION

PART III: NOW WHAT?

IT TAKES MORE EFFORT TO BE

D'SoRGANIZED

THAN IT DOES TO BE

ORGANIZED

ABOUT THIS BOOK

WHY YOU NEED TO READ THIS BOOK

Do you . . .

1. Tell yourself it's just this week that is disorganized, and next week will be better?

2. Wake up in the morning with a subconscious sense of dread, wondering who or what you're going to forget today?

3. Go to bed at night making lists in your head for the next day, only to forget half of it by morning?

4. Know that there must be an easier way to the Land of the Organized, but your GPS won't tell you how to get there?

5. Keep on buying pretty containers to get organized and then continually trip over them as they gather dust in the corner, because you aren't quite sure how best to use them?

Good. I'm liking you already.

The goal of this book is to show you how to fit more of what you love into each day. Now, I know that "being organized" can sound as intimidating as it sounds unattainable. I am here to quell your fear of being organized and show you how time and space management are first cousins of money management: Just as a financially savvy person enjoys monetary security and freedom, if you use your time wisely, you will be able to lead a life of time-managed freedom. I will tell you nothing about how to arrange your cans in ABC order, but I will tell you how to arrange your life so that you can do what you love.

The bottom line is this: It is taking you more effort to be disorganized than it would to be organized.

Systems are the key to a more organized, relaxed life. Think for a moment about the traffic light. It is a simple, elegant system that is recognized all over the world, keeping drivers in every country safe and organized. Imagine the dangers if one town decided to give its traffic light system a makeover and introduced seven different colors, each using a different system for delivering instructions. Less dramatically, consider the chaos and confusion that usually results from a broken traffic light.

Systemized living is just like the traffic light. Minimal thinking, no anxiety, and a system you can count on, allowing you to focus your mind on the stuff that matters most. This book provides examples and ideas for how to create systems and smarter ways to accomplish your day-to-day responsibilities and to provide what your family needs from you in the most effective manner. Having these systems in place will reduce your anxiety and free up more time for you to spend on what you love doing and on the things that really matter to you. That, in turn, will recharge your batteries, and you will be happier, less stressed, and more fun to be around again. (You will also have fewer frown lines, and your children won't need therapy when they grow up.) Talk about a quantifiable win-win situation.

~*~

Forever—is composed of nows.

—EMILY DICKINSON

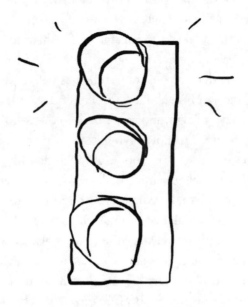

A SIMPLE SYSTEM
RESPECTED
THE WORLD OVER

HOW TO USE THIS BOOK

How you use this book is entirely your call. (If you must use it as a doorstop, go ahead—but please don't tell me.) This book was written with the overwhelmed, stretched-too-thin, sleep-deprived mom in mind. So feel free to read it from start to finish, or to just flip it open to a random page. Not everything in these pages will speak to you; however, I hope that some essential themes will. If you are having a really rough day (and we all have those on occasion), just look at the illustrations, have a laugh, and come back to the words another time.

And I promise, I'm not leaving you on your own here, either. Many of the themes in this book are included in more detail on my website (www.sobeorganized.com), where you will find lots of additional tips and tools to help you on your path to systemization, as well as my regular blog on all things organized. Because we moms take strength from each other, I have also created a Frazzled to Focused Facebook page where you can ask for advice, share ideas, or just vent! And if you just haven't gotten enough of me by then, please follow me on my So Be Organized Facebook page and on Twitter (@sobeorganized).

It's what you think you know that will

prevent you from learning.

—ANONYMOUS

THE TOOLS YOU NEED

In order to get started, you will need a few basic "tools":

1. **An Open Mind.** The most important item you can bring to this process is an open mind. As Einstein said, the definition of insanity is "doing the same thing over and over again and expecting different results." Allowing yourself to envision doing things differently is a formidable gift you can give to yourself.

2. **A Time Out for Yourself.** Now that you've opened your mind, the vital next step is to commit to taking some time alone in a quiet place to start strategizing. You can't possibly think over anything remotely serious with the little guys asking you eighty-seven questions simultaneously.

3. **A Place to Write It All Down.** Goodwill alone will not match up your children's socks or brush their teeth. So you need to have some place other than your brain to store all your plans and ideas. It can be an actual paper planner, an iPad, or a notebook—it just shouldn't be a bunch of random sticky notes or the backs of envelopes.

OK. Are you ready? Let's get started . . .

PART I

GETTING IT ALL

TOGETHER

∦ 1 ∦

FREE YOUR MIND

LOVING THE MORE ORGANIZED YOU

MOST people—you may be one of them—feel some initial resistance to the concept of a *system*. The very word conjures up images of assembly lines that stifle creativity and a dull gray existence from now until eternity. But here's the good news: The systems you are going to create are custom-made for your life, for your family's unique likes, dislikes, and lifestyle. They will help you do things smarter, simpler, and better. The beauty is that once you begin to systemize parts of your life, you free up precious time and brain cells that you were wasting reinventing the wheel over and over again.

Develop a healthy disregard for the impossible.

—LARRY PAGE, COFOUNDER OF GOOGLE

Obviously not everything will fit well into a system. I don't advocate systemizing the exact order in which you play Lego with your child or the conversation topics for your date nights with your husband (though the *schedule* of date nights could be systemized). But there is no reason why you should come home every night and wonder what to make for dinner, only to find that you don't have the ingredients to make what you finally decide upon.

SWITCHING FROM DOING IT ALL TO DOING MOST OF IT (AND KNOWING THAT THAT'S OK)

It takes some time and some failed attempts at being Supermom to realize that being a good mom is not about doing it all, just as going to a good restaurant is not about ordering every dish on the menu. The key to success is to prioritize tasks and decide that you will do only what you *really* need (or want) to do—and then to figure out how to do those things smarter.

Your first reaction to that may be: Well, I *need* to do it all. A mother's nature by default is that we want to do it all (or feel that we *have* to do it all). We always have to drive the kids ourselves, make the dinner with our own two hands, and fold their socks just right. However, I'm here to tell you that that's not actually true. Yes, there are things that just have to get done, and some of them have to get done by you. But there are also plenty of things you do every day that could be done differently, or be done by someone else, or just not be done at all.

So, with only twenty-four hours in a day, and the need to sleep for at least some of those hours, how do you work out what doesn't actually have to be done by you? You first need to make peace with the fact that while wanting to do it all ourselves is very natural, it doesn't always yield the returns we envision. Car pools get delayed, carefully prepared dinners get vetoed by the kids, and the snuggly bedtime story turns into the mental torture of "How am I going to get through this book without falling asleep before my child?"

We have to internalize the notion that we truly can't do it all. And that that is OK.

THERE IS **NO REASON**
YOU SHOULD COME
HOME EVERY NIGHT
AND WONDER WHAT

TO MAKE FOR DINNER

GETTING YOURSELF PSYCHED UP FOR CHANGE

The most influential person who will talk to you all day is you, so you should be very careful about what you say to you.

— ZIG ZIGLAR

Change is easy. You go first.

Actually, truth be told, we are all scared of change. Even little changes can throw us for a loop. Try holding your phone with the other hand or driving the children to school along a different route. It can be quite unnerving. However, when you have to change phone hands because you sprained your wrist or when a broken water pipe causes a detour on the way to school, you do survive. While the initial learning curve can be quite steep, it usually works out—and sometimes you may even end up preferring the new way of doing things. It is the same with learning to live life in a more organized fashion.

Forging a new path toward a more systemized life can be quite overwhelming psychologically. So it is important to constantly remind yourself of your good intentions, and not let your mind scare you into not believing in your ideas. Pin up a photo of yourself using your slow cooker for the first time or keep a motivational quote that makes you smile on the screensaver of your phone. Be as creative or as boring as you like, but take the time to surround yourself with positive thoughts and images. Just as someone on a diet might visualize her "skinny self," make sure you have a vision of your more organized self to encourage you to start thinking in a more efficient manner.

And wish as we might, the tangible changes in our lives are

going to start slowly. You won't be feeling super organized within a month. Your dinners might be written neatly on a weekly meal chart, but you may still need to tweak the corresponding grocery list, and when you've finally cracked the code on the grocery list, you may realize that your basement is still a dump. Your taxes are filed, but your kids still don't know what they're supposed to wear to school the next day. It is a slow, yet sustainable process, one that will be frustrating at times and quite exhilarating at others.

It may help to think about being on a six-lane highway. You are in the far left lane and you need to get all the way over to the right. Your only solution is to move over one lane at a time. So don't get frustrated when you've been working hard and have shifted over only one lane; it truly is a process. And quite often the tricks you use to get from one lane to the other can be transferred when you need to change lanes again. So enjoy the cumulative gains, and remember that the basic goal is to stay on the road.

OVERCOMING MOM'S THREE CLASSIC PSYCHOLOGICAL HURDLES

Life's problems wouldn't be called "hurdles" if there wasn't a way to get over them.

—RANDY PAUSCH

Even with all the best intentions and positive thinking, there are a few obstacles we all run into at one time or another. As I talk about them below, they probably will sound kind of familiar. It is likely that you faced them in school or that you see them every day at work. Whether you realize it or not, they are also affecting you at home.

The Evil Twins: Perfectionism & Procrastination

It is important to resist the false lure of *perfectionism* in your day-to-day life. Here is the truth: Not everything has to be perfect. Seriously.

The majority of the tasks that come our way can be accomplished very well with an 85–95 percent success rate. In fact, doing everything at a 105-percent level is a huge waste of time and energy. Living life with perfectionist standards is the emotional equivalent of choosing to walk between two buildings on a tightrope, rather than simply walking across the street. It's dangerous, highly risky, and fraught with anxiety for yourself and all those around you.

It is essential to *selectively* lower that bar and reserve the laser-beam focus for when you really need it.

If you are the person responsible for packing my parachute before I jump out of an airplane, then I certainly hope you pay incredibly close attention to detail. However, I hope you don't hold your five-year-old child's bed-making skills to the same standard. Choosing the person you marry or the house you live in or your child's name are examples of decisions for which you should exercise perfectionist standards. However, the food you pack for your children's lunch, the cleanliness of your outdoor garbage cans, or how carefully you fold your shirts can be very good or even just good if you are investing your energy in other, more worthy endeavors.

The decision to become more human—less perfect—is not an easy one to make, despite the fact that we know we have been trying to accomplish the impossible.

—ANN W. SMITH

THE EVIL TWINS

PERFECTIONISM

PROCRASTINATION

Procrastination is the evil twin of perfectionism. When you procrastinate, the subliminal message you are sending yourself is "If I can't do this perfectly right now, then I'm not going to bother doing it today at all." While this may seem to be a logical thought at first, perfectionism and procrastination continue to feed off each other in a vicious cycle that prevents us from doing the things we need or want to do. It also takes up a huge amount of mental energy. It is time to get back to appreciating the beauty of *good* and save *perfect* for when you really need it.

A good plan executed now is better than an excellent plan executed never.

—ANONYMOUS

Prioritizing Those Priorities

Time must be guarded. Every moment that passes isn't just a "moment," but a piece of your life.

—HAYOM YOM

Lack of time is actually a lack of priorities. No matter how manic your schedule, if you won the lottery you would unquestionably drop everything and run off to claim your gazillion-dollar check.

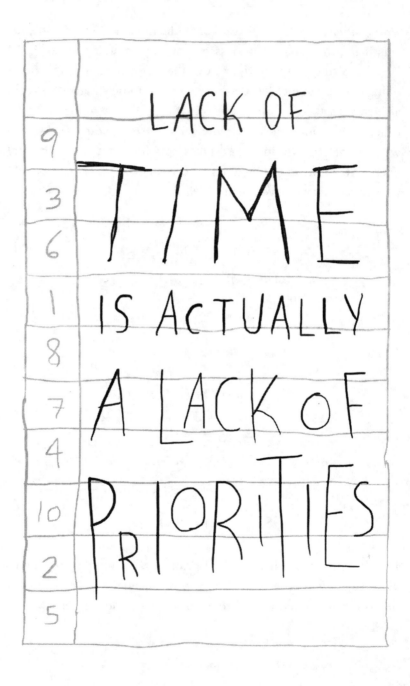

LACK OF TIME IS ACTUALLY A LACK OF PRIORITIES

Ask anyone you know how they are, and chances are part of the answer will include the word "busy." We are all busy, busy, busy. But what are we actually doing? When you finally get the kids in bed and collapse on the sofa with a sigh because it was *such a busy day*, do you ever wonder what exactly it was that kept you so busy?

Some people run around being busy, but don't move closer to their goals, so essentially they are just being busy on the treadmill of life without actually going anywhere. It is all well and good to be super busy, helping your friends move, running a bake sale at school, or helping a neighbor plant a garden. But it is important to make sure you can afford the expenditure of time required to do these things.

Getting back to the idea of not being able to do it all—and remember: *Doing it all is an illusion*—we need to learn to prioritize all the priorities clamoring for our attention. You may have a million things to do, but not everything needs your immediate attention. Not having a clear sense of what your top priorities are will lead you to focus on the wrong things, at the expense of your valuable time and sanity.

The Vital Difference Between Effective & Efficient

Doing something unimportant well

does not make it important.

—TIM FERRISS

There is one life skill you really have to understand, digest, and apply to your world, so pay attention: It is as essential to be able to differentiate between effective and efficient as it is to be able to spot a fake handbag across a room.

Effective means getting another step closer to producing the intended or expected result. *Efficient* means doing something in the best possible way, with the least waste of time and effort.

Yes, it is good to be efficient, but only if you are doing the *right things* efficiently. Doing something that is not a top priority efficiently does not bring you closer to your goal of living a more organized and low-stress life. It doesn't matter so much *how* you do something if *what* you are doing is not what you should be doing. However, doing the top things on your "to do" list *effectively* will bring you closer to your goals.

ENERGY LEVELS

⋇

I'm most creative from five to nine a.m.
If I had a boss or coworkers, they would ruin
my best hours one way or another.
—SCOTT ADAMS, CREATOR OF DILBERT

One way to increase your effectiveness is to figure out when you work best. Are you a night owl? An early bird? A hybrid of the two, depending on your caffeine intake and any imminent deadlines? Learn how to make your energy levels work for you by carving out focused time in the hours when you are most alert and can get the most work done uninterrupted.

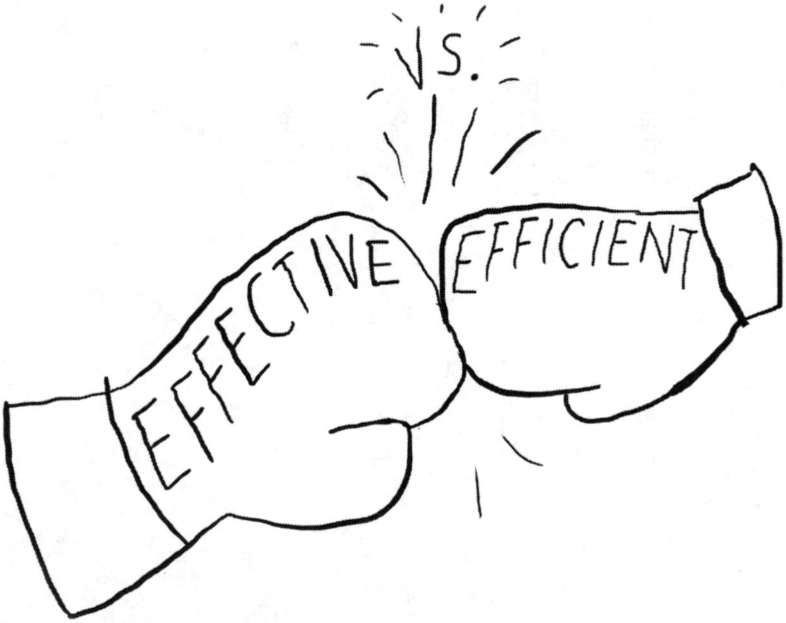
VS.
EFFECTIVE
EFFICIENT

2

SETTING PRIORITIES

LESS IS MORE (MORE OR LESS . . .)

*With so many opportunities
and so many constraints, successfully picking
what to do next is your moment of
highest leverage. It deserves more time and
attention than most people give it.*

—SETH GODIN

BEFORE we talk about the mechanics of systemization, I want to review some basic concepts of time management that will help you decide what items need your love now and which resilient fellows can wait until the clocks change. These tried and tested concepts are guaranteed to make things run more smoothly—if you choose to apply them (a bit like that eye cream you bought last week).

THE ECONOMICS OF MOTHERHOOD

You want to do it all because that is how we moms are wired. It's the heart-pumping adrenaline rush of the fight-or-flight response. However, not everything is worth a bout of self-induced hysteria. Choking hazards should get your blood flowing; being a bit late for a ballet class should not. When we put everything in the "urgent" category, we become depleted, out of whack, and—most relevant— unable to concentrate on what matters most.

Your time is finite and precious.
Say "no" to requests from others before you
say "no" to time with your kids.

—DR. HARLEY ROTBART

It may seem that you can just choose whatever is on the top of the pile and start with that. You know the old adage about the squeaky wheel getting the grease. However, the squeaky wheel might be just a little noisy, while the other wheels are about to fall off their axles.

What you choose to focus on really does matter; it will have a cumulative impact on everything that follows.

The following time management tips can help you figure out what those things should be. You may recognize a few of them from Economics 101. Turns out that stuff really was relevant to your daily life!

The 80/20 Rule

Look at your shoes—80 percent of the shoes you selected to wear last month came from 20 percent of the shoes you own. How about your kids' toys? Yes, you guessed it—20 percent of the toys probably account for about 80 percent of the playtime.

THE ECONOMIC$ OF MOTHERHOOD

Vilfredo Pareto would agree with you. He was an early-twentieth-century economist who observed that 80 percent of the property in Italy was owned by 20 percent of the population. As it happened, he also noticed that the same rule applied to the peas in his garden: 20 percent of the pea pods contained 80 percent of the peas. As he began to apply this rule to other areas of his life, he found that it continued to stand true. This observation was later generalized into the Pareto Principle, also called the 80/20 rule.

In plain English, the 80/20 rule is as follows: 80 percent of outcomes arise from 20 percent of inputs; in other words, 80 percent of results come from 20 percent of your time and effort.

Apply this principle to your time management issues: What 20 percent of sources are causing 80 percent of your problems? What 20 percent of sources are causing 80 percent of your happiness?

Are you getting the idea? The 20 percent that is causing you the most headaches is earning a spot at the top of your priority list. And the 20 percent that gives you the most happiness needs to be prioritized too.

Opportunity Costs

Instead of reading this book, you could be doing approximately one million different things. The same applies to other aspects of your life; there will always be other things you could be doing at the very moment you are doing something else.

Opportunity cost is the foregone value of the alternative you didn't choose. In economics, it is often expressed in money, but in life, opportunity cost can also take the form of lost chances, lost pleasure, lost time, or undesired consequences.

The basic lesson is that when it comes to deciding what gets your attention, you must make sure it is a worthwhile investment.

The key opportunity-cost questions to ask yourself are:

What would happen if this area, project, or issue were ignored altogether?

Can I wait a few days, weeks, or months to focus on it?

Can it be given to someone else to do?

If the answers to these questions include phrases such as "absolute mayhem" or "my children would go to school in their underwear" or "my brain would explode," then clearly those things are high priorities. However, if the answers are more along the lines of "it wouldn't be so bad" or "it doesn't really matter" or "whatever," then maybe these are things you can delay, outsource, or ignore altogether.

Parkinson's Law

Parkinson's Law states that "work expands to fill the time available for its completion." Simply put, this is the magic of the imminent deadline. There is nothing better than the arrival of out-of-town guests, an upcoming birthday party, or a graduate school paper that is due in three days to get your mind focused and working at twenty-six times its usual pace. If you have three weeks to get something done, you will spend three weeks worrying about it and stressing over it while you get it done. If you have only three days, you will still get it done, but with a whole lot less worry and stress.

So whenever possible, if there is something you need to get done but have been putting off, set an imminent deadline for the completion of the activity. Give yourself organizational deadlines that coincide with events in your home or your life. The essential question to ask yourself is: How can I back this up to start the process even earlier than usual? If you make a consistent habit of not taking the real deadline seriously and constantly make your own (earlier) deadline, you will reduce your stress level tremendously, because *last-minute problems are a lot easier to take care of when they aren't actually happening at the last minute.*

DO, DELEGATE, DELETE

A first step in setting priorities is to do a mental brain dump. First, take the time to write all of those "to do's" on a big piece of paper (or on your iPad or on your wall). Do this step away from all children who could distract you. Also, improve your focus by not having background noise if that annoys you, and turn the ringer on your phone off.

Wherever you are writing this list, make three long columns and label them:

Do   **Delegate**   **Delete**

As you go through this book you will find ways in which to *do* the things on your list smarter. You will learn to give yourself permission to *delegate* effectively and in some instances creatively, and you will give yourself permission to simply *delete* certain items.

Now start to list everything you do, everything you wish you were doing, and everything that's on your mind. You will feel your anxiety level rise as you mentally chastise yourself for not having completed everything on this list already. Ignore this feeling; just keep on writing. The goal here is to get every little item out of your mind. Write down e-v-e-r-y-t-h-i-n-g that is rattling around in your head.

Remember, right now it is the *what*, not the *how*. It is not about finding the perfect solution; you'll be more adept at doing that once you have benefited from the tools in this book. The goal now is simply to identify what needs to be done, what is holding you back from being organized, what needs to be delegated to someone else, and what needs to be deleted altogether.

Be honest with yourself. What is *not* getting done but *should* be getting done? What should you be delegating that you are too stubborn (sorry, but we need to be honest here) to let go of? You

DO	DELEGATE	DELETE

should delegate the items that are loathsome to you, those whose opportunity costs are too high, or those that someone else could do just as well—or well enough.

I know you have no idea *how* you are going to outsource certain key items at the moment, and there are no magic answers that apply to everyone, but by taking the step of putting certain items in the *delegate* column, you are freeing up your mind to start considering other options. Also, be realistic about the things you really should not be worrying about until your kids are out of diapers or in school or driving or in college or married or supporting you in your old age. Finally, feel free to add in a few goals that seem highly irrational for such a busy mom.

You will soon learn that there is time for you to be responsible, supplement your income, and dream big. So go ahead and write down your dream of planting an organic vegetable garden or taking tennis lessons; we will make time for that.

***

You will never "find" time for anything. If you want time, you must make it.

—CHARLES BUXTON

This initial brain dump should take about thirty to forty-five minutes. After that, put it someplace safe, away from marker-wielding toddlers, and keep adding items as you go through your week, living your regular life. You are essentially creating a working document to replace your brain. There is no right or wrong way to do this. Just keep on pulling items out of your mind and putting them on paper (or on the screen or the wall).

Don't worry too much about getting the column placement exactly right. These lists are not carved in stone; you can move things around from column to column, tomorrow or next week or next month. If you're not sure where something goes, put it in the *do* column. As you go through this book, you may find ways to move it to *delegate* or *delete*, or you may decide that you actually should be doing it yourself.

CREATING YOUR "TO DON'T" LIST: MY HEART SAYS YES, BUT MY CALENDAR SAYS NO

Now take a look at your three columns. The items in the *do* column are obviously your "to do" list. Which makes the items in the *delegate* and *delete* columns your "to don't" list. This list is just as important as your "to do" list, if not more so. You need to give yourself permission to let go of some things and realize that the world will still continue to spin. At the end of the day, you will be a much calmer and more pleasant mother, wife, sister, daughter, friend, or employee if you can do this.

Remember: *A "to do" list can be overwhelming. A "to don't" list is life-changing!* Just because something is on your "to don't" list doesn't mean it is never going to get done. It can be outsourced, it can be delegated, it can be delayed until a more realistic time. It is just not going to get done *by you at this particular moment in time.*

The first step toward successfully embracing your "to don't" list is learning to say no. In today's "yes" world, we need to cultivate a proud notion of "no." You see, if everything is important, then nothing is important, and we have already determined that working smarter isn't about doing absolutely everything at 20 percent; it is about doing the predetermined items at 90–100 percent. So stop feeling obliged to say yes and start being protective of the key priorities in your world.

CREATE YOUR...

TO **DON'T** LIST

~~MAKE 73 PECAN PIES~~

~~LEARN JAPANESE~~

~~READ ENCYCLOPEDIA~~

~~CLIMB MOUNTAIN~~

Another part of embracing the culture of "to don't" is to stop trying to cram more into every moment. Sometimes we erroneously think that by working more hours and pushing harder and harder we will get ahead of the curve. Nothing could be further from the truth. We need to switch off and be present in the lives of our family, recharge, reboot, and then go back to work with a clear mind.

DELEGATING MORE EFFECTIVELY TO YOUR "STAFF"

Life is too short for you to spend it doing things you find toxic. That is why you need to learn to delegate.

I know. I hear you. You are still asking, But whom am I going to outsource to? You may not have a maid and a butler, but whatever your income, we all have "staff." You are most likely not washing every dish by hand, and you're probably not pounding your dirty clothes on rocks in the river. Your dishwasher, your washing machine, your dryer, your freezer, your slow cooker, and the preset button on your oven are all already working together to make your life more manageable. The trick is to use these "employees" and others to make it even easier. Create rock-solid laundry systems that don't involve using your mind and rock-star dinners that involve your delegation team and take the guesswork and frustration out of cooking, and you will free yourself up to spend your time having more fun and less stress.

Involve the kids; they are your cheapest

source of labor.

—PETE WALSH

You will also find that there actually are people in your life to whom you can delegate very effectively: your husband, your parents, the babysitter, a friend, a neighbor, even your kids. There are lots of things that people can help you with, ways to share the burden and creative ways to outsource. Does the thought of ironing give you hives? Barter with a friend who doesn't mind ironing, and watch her kids for an hour in exchange. Still no luck? Call a local ironing service and eat macaroni and cheese for an extra night if budgeting is tight.

It will be much easier to delegate if you allow yourself to lower your high standards once in a while. Now I'm not saying that your kids need to bathe only once a month, but there probably are a few places you could give a little. Sometimes we end up with too much on our plates because we insist we are the only one who can do something a certain way.

Admit it: You have doubts that your husband can effectively make dinner for the kids, supervise homework, and keep the house from being declared a hazardous waste zone. But you know what? He can. Did you ever go away for a while, on a girls' weekend or a business trip or even for the afternoon? When you got back, were the kids starving, half-dressed, and lost in piles of garbage? Probably not.

HITTING THAT DELETE BUTTON (GO ON . . . YOU CAN DO IT)

The art of the art is picking your limits.

That's the autonomy I most cherish.

The freedom to pick my boundaries.

—SETH GODIN

You already know many of the items that should be deleted. You just feel bad about them, because they have been on your "to do" list for so long.

Did you overextend yourself and commit to taking a cake-decorating class with a friend, only to realize that you would really prefer to take an exercise class instead? Delete.

Did you volunteer to pack bags at your local organic co-op, but consistently miss your Tuesday morning shift because you have a two-year-old and an infant and are volunteering three years too early? Delete.

How about the book you started but are reading only because your best friend loved it? Or the book club you really don't have any interest in but feel you should go to? Delete.

Organizing the garden shed in labeled plastic containers? Delete.

It might be tempting at this point to delete a little more responsibility than you really should. Keep in mind the time management equivalent of "floss only the teeth you want to keep." There may be tasks that fill you with dread but that still need to get done one way or another. Delete what can be deleted without dire consequences and do and delegate the items that you want to see continuing to improve in your life.

HIT THAT

delete

BUTTON

Remember, just because something is in the *delete* column doesn't mean it is gone forever. So stop feeling guilty. When your kids are a bit older, maybe you'll go back to the organic co-op. When you have a little more time, maybe you will organize the shed. But at the moment, let's focus on key priorities and get your anxiety down and your productivity up. Once you've done that, you can choose to slowly bring back items from the *delete* column to *do* or *delegate*.

SO WHAT DO I DO TODAY (AND TOMORROW, AND THE NEXT DAY . . .)?

Now let's apply all this wisdom to what you will do on a day-to-day basis. Each week, choose the items from your "to do" list that you will focus on during the following week. It might help to divide these items into columns representing each of your major roles. For example, let's say you are a mother of two children, vice president of the PTA, a part-time psychologist, and somewhat of a caregiver to your parents, who live twenty minutes away. Your weekly tasks would be divided into four columns: Children, PTA, Work, and Mom & Dad. Some of the tasks on your list will be the same from week to week (grocery shopping, taking a child to a weekly appointment, your yoga class), and some will change each week (buying new shoes for your daughter, making calls for the PTA, finishing a report for work, a dentist appointment).

After you have chosen the items you will focus on during a particular week, each night choose five to eight key items that *must* be done the next day. I strongly recommend using a planner pad, smartphone app of your choice, or even an index card to keep track of these key items. Apply the time management skills and concepts you have already learned to determine what does and does not belong on that daily list.

By identifying ahead of time where your focus lies, you will instantly become more productive. When you have eight minutes free, you will be able to check off item #1, rather than checking the *Huffington Post* or your Facebook page. While certainly less entertaining, ticking off these items will help point you toward your goal of working smarter and reducing stress.

CHOOSE HAPPINESS

A Happy Mom Is a Happy Family

While you are in the midst of setting priorities, remember that one of the most important choices you can make is choosing to be happy. Therefore, it is OK to put something on your "to do" list just because it makes you happy. And maybe you should reconsider one or two of the items that you relegated to the *delete* list just because their sole virtue was making you happy.

Life is so much more complicated when we are grouchy. Research shows that optimism can be learned, so here's a quick lesson on bringing more meaning and happiness into your world.

Happiness and leading a meaningful life are connected. In his best-selling book, *Man's Search for Meaning*, Viktor Frankl introduced logotherapy, which is based on the idea that the search for meaning in life is the most powerful motivation for human behavior. After witnessing firsthand the horrors of Auschwitz, as both inmate and psychiatrist, Frankl understood that when we find meaning in our lives, we can survive the most challenging of experiences.

If a prisoner felt that he could no longer endure the realities of camp life, he found a way out in his mental life—an invaluable opportunity to dwell in the spiritual domain, the one that the SS was unable to destroy. Spiritual life strengthened the prisoner, helped him adapt, and thereby improved his chances of survival.

Frankl often said that, even within the narrow boundaries of the concentration camps, he found only two kinds of men: decent ones and unprincipled ones. This held true through all classes, ethnicities, and nationalities.

Psychologist Martin Seligman took this concept further and created positive psychology, which encourages people to stop focusing on what is wrong and concentrate on how to be a happier and more functional person. In Dr. Seligman's theory, the "good life" consists of five elements:

1. **P**ositive emotions (pleasure, warmth, comfort, etc.)
2. **E**ngagement (or flow, absorption in an enjoyed yet challenging activity)
3. **R**elationships (social ties, an extremely reliable indicator of happiness)
4. **M**eaning (a perceived quest or belonging to something bigger)
5. **A**ccomplishments (having realized tangible goals).

Time has a way of slipping through our fingers, and often the things we do for ourselves get lost in the shuffle of the things we do for everyone else. The Pilates class that makes you feel so good gets pushed lower on the totem pole than the bike, cheese, or vitamins you need to buy for your child, dog, or goat. But you will regret missing that class and it will get you down. So go ahead and designate certain items as nonnegotiable, which means that aside from the school calling you to pick up your child immediately, you will take care of what makes you happy and grounded, and then fit everything else in around it.

⹔ 3 ⹔

CLEARING OUT
THE CLUTTER

STREAMLINE YOUR HOME & YOUR HEAD

Simplicity is the ultimate sophistication.

—LEONARDO DA VINCI

*It seems that perfection is reached not when there
is nothing left to add, but when there is nothing
left to take away.*

—ANTOINE DE SAINT-EXUPÉRY

NOW that you've spent all that time and energy prioritizing your priorities, don't complicate things. In order to do things smarter and better and implement rock-solid systems that work, you need to simplify both your mental and physical spaces to be able to achieve the focus you need. This means limiting the things surrounding you, limiting your choices, limiting your information input. In this section, I will help you get past the psychological barriers to a streamlined environment and a streamlined mind.

AVOIDING DECISION OVERLOAD

Quite simply, you need to streamline your world, because you will go crazy if you don't. *You need to limit your choices so you are not paralyzed by them.* Fewer choices will enable you to make decisions more easily and more intelligently, so you can lower your stress and focus on what matters.

From choosing new shoes for the children or buying a new phone to dinner plans and travel reservations, there is no avoiding decision making in our lives. In his book *The Paradox of Choice*, psychologist Dr. Barry Schwartz explains that today we live with an unprecedented number of choices in almost all arenas of life. As an example, he encourages his readers to count how many different types of salad dressings are offered on the shelves of an average supermarket. By his last count, it's more than four hundred.

This ridiculous amount of choice leads to "paralysis by analysis," in which there is no clear winner. Dr. Schwartz's research has shown that an abundance of choices leads to more confusion and less satisfaction. He defines *maximizers* as people who, when given a choice, will search all the possible information sources in order to make the best possible choice. Maximizers tend to have lingering, nagging doubts and a high level of negativity. *Satisficers*, on the other hand, make an "OK" decision with minimal amounts of information and are happier.

—⁂—

It is impossible to have perfect and complete information at any given time to make a decision.

— HERBERT SIMON

(who won a Nobel Prize for his contribution to organizational decision making)

Simplifying your mental and physical space will make everything you do easier. If you have fewer choices, it will be easier to make a decision. If you have fewer items in your closet, it will be easier to get dressed every day. If you have only three water bottles instead of twenty-five, it will be easier to choose one on your way out the door. I could go on and on, but I don't want to complicate things.

A CLUTTERED SPACE IS A CLUTTERED MIND

Look around at your home, your car, your office, your yard. What do you see? How many of those things do you use on a regular basis? How many have you been planning to get rid of, but just haven't gotten around to tossing?

A key first step in streamlining your world is to clear out your physical environment by defeating the clutter that threatens to overwhelm us all. This involves a commitment to cutting down on the unnecessary things that are cluttering up the world around you and impeding your ability to work smarter and get things done.

You do realize that, when you were young and your mom asked you to please tidy your room, it had nothing to do with teaching you values and responsibility right? It was because the clutter in your bedroom upstairs was making her crazy as she was getting work done downstairs. Even though she couldn't actually *see* the clutter, it was silently driving her insane, and that's because *clear space is essential for clear thinking.* You were blocking her thought process.

You probably understand that feeling now. Say your front patio is cluttered with a once-pretty but now fully mildewed chair that no one sits on and that is used only to hold bike helmets. Every time you walk by that chair, it makes you crazy. That chair is zapping your energy and cluttering your mind. Maybe you don't have a mildewing chair on your front patio. Maybe you don't even have a

A CLUTTERED SPACE

IS A

CLUTTERED MIND

front patio. Just insert whichever broken, rotting, or obsolete item is haunting you every time you pass it.

Clutter is just a pile of delayed decision making. It makes our shoulders tense and gives us the unconscious notion that we don't have a handle on the fundamentals of our lives. Listen loud and listen clear: Get rid of your clutter. It is going to suck the happiness and empowerment out of your day.

Clutter stops us from living in the present.

—PETE WALSH

PRACTICAL SOLUTIONS FOR OUTSMARTING CLUTTER

Clutter follows the same basic rules as matter. Nothing ever truly goes away; it simply changes form. So you need to be militant about moving the clutter out of your front door. Develop a healthy obsession with garbage cans, and use these tips to help you finally conquer that clutter and free up your physical and mental space.

Give Items Away. Clearing out the clutter can not only reduce your stress, it can help make a real difference in someone else's life. If you don't need it or aren't using it, there is someone out there who does need it and will use it. Stop looking at clutter as a negative thing; turn the situation on its head and embrace it as a golden opportunity to do something positive.

If your children are old enough, this is also a great chance to teach them about giving. Involve your kids in the process of sorting through things and deciding what you don't need or aren't using. Take them with you to the shelter, thrift shop, or drop-off point and let them see that their old things will have a new life with someone else. This is a powerful lesson for kids.

Switch from Just in Case to Just Enough. For some reason, we all have the instinct to stockpile things "just in case." But if we want our homes to feel uncluttered and we want to strive for the notion of "everything in its place," then the very first goal should be to have fewer items. Now, I know what you're thinking. And it is true that, once in a while, the things we hold on to do come in handy. But was it worth the space and stress they caused in the meantime? As an alternative, adopt the "just enough" mentality. Keep the items you *love* or those that are incredibly useful, and pass on the items that don't fall into those categories. The upside of this is that you will have fewer items in your home to manage, every item will have its place, and you will have a clearer mind. The downside is that every once in a while you will need to buy or borrow a bottle warmer or a stroller for guests.

There are two ways of going through life: Gather everything in sight, just in case you need it. Or trust you'll find exactly what you need, just in time. Guess which one lets you really stop and smell the roses?

— MARTHA BECK

Respect the Life Span. Everything from the robin singing in your garden to your car to the new shoes you bought last month has a life span. When you have possessions and their time is up, be kind and allow them to exit gracefully. Alternatively, give them a makeover to help them last an additional few years. The dried-flower arrangement from your wedding may have been a romantic reminder of your special day, but it has now been twelve years, and it looks awful sitting there on your dresser. Let it go, and fill the space with a happy photo from your wedding day instead.

Understand the "Clutter Inheritance Tax." Sometimes, we have items stuck in our home as part of the clutter, because they were a gift. This can be something like the "interesting" vase that you got as a housewarming present or a dresser that your late aunt gave you. You may feel trapped into keeping these things; you think the responsible thing to do is to take care of it, especially if it was inherited from a loved one (and particularly if that loved one has passed away). The first step in receiving a gift is to thank the giver. Once you have sincerely communicated your appreciation for their thought, time, and energy, your responsibility to the giver ends. After that, the item is yours to do whatever you want with. You are free to exchange it, re-gift it, repurpose it, or give it away. (Unless, of course, it is the priceless family jewels that have been handed down to the oldest daughter for fifteen generations. You really should keep those.)

One In, One Out. When you were out shopping, did you find a pair of Tom's espadrilles that you couldn't live without? By all means, buy them and enjoy them. But make sure you pass on another pair of shoes from your closet—one that hasn't seen the light of day in years. (Remember the 80/20 rule.) Same too for sweaters, gloves, swimsuits, children's toys, and many, many other things.

Let the Mistakes Swim on By. Let's say you bought a pair of $120 shoes that pinch your toes and make you feel like an irresponsible person every time you see them. Barter them with a friend, send them to a consignment store, or give them to your sister. Just stop keeping them in your closet simply to punish yourself. You are not going to wear them if they are that uncomfortable. Same for the pan you bought at full price that burns soups because the metal is so thin or the cute chair you bought for the children without thinking about whether it could be washed (it couldn't). We all make mistakes. So commit to losing those reminders of your mistakes. You've learned the lesson; you don't need to live in a museum displaying proof of all of your errors.

THINGS TO GET RID OF NOW

- Any shirt with stains under the arms
- Any book that makes you feel bad about yourself
- Any package of food that has been open for more than two months
- Magazines you've already read, twice
- Spices from two years ago
- Clothes that make you feel bad about your body
- Linens and towels that you wouldn't want to use
- Any broken appliance that would cost more to repair than to replace
- Any items that friends have asked you to store for them— give them back!
- Clothing that is not your size
- Shoes that have been worn through and cannot be repaired

CLEARING OUT THE MENTAL CLUTTER: DECIDE TO DECIDE SMARTER

Worrying is like a rocking chair. It gives you something to do, but it doesn't actually get you anywhere.

—ANONYMOUS

Just as clearing out the physical clutter will allow you to find things more easily and give you space to breathe, clearing out your mental clutter by limiting information input and choices will free you to think more clearly about important things, save you time you would have spent worrying about less important stuff, and help you make decisions more intelligently, quickly, and easily. Your brain has the capacity to store everything you see, hear, or read in your lifetime. The real challenge is in accessing the specific information you need when you need it. Think how much easier it will be to "find" things in your mind if there is not a lot of extraneous information cluttering it up.

Even if you limit your information input, you are still going to have to make lots and lots of decisions. The more strategies you have to deal with these decisions, the simpler it is going to be for you. Use the following tips, combined with your new, streamlined mind, to take the stress out of much of your daily decision making:

Trust Your Gut Instinct. Did you ever have a doctor, teacher, or other expert tell you your child was fine when you were absolutely certain something was amiss? Were you right? There's a reason they call it mother's intuition. You may not have a medical degree or a PhD in psychology, but you are very often the best judge of what your children and your family need at any given time. The same is true for yourself and your decision-making challenges. You can do all the research you like, but your first, "gut" choice is often the right one. It's kind of like buying the first dress you tried on and loved. You can spend all day shopping for the perfect outfit, only to wind up heading back to the first store you visited, minutes before closing time, to buy that very first dress you tried on. If you had just bought it that morning, think about all the time and stress you would have saved yourself! There are two types of gut instinct: innate (those instances where you "just know") and learned (the product of years of cumulative decision making and lessons learned). Whichever type is acting at any given moment, listen to that clever inner voice that is whispering in your ear. She is very frequently right.

Focus Your Thinking. Give yourself the best shot at making the right decisions by making them when your mind is at its clearest. Resist making decisions when you are distracted, unfocused, or cranky. Some people do well mulling things over while they walk, drive, or exercise. And there's always the shower. Figure out when and where works best for you. Make a note of specific decisions that need your attention and plug them in to a specific time and place.

Outsource Decisions. Take the pain out of decision making altogether by not making certain decisions. Instead, ask people with a deeper knowledge in certain areas. In your car-pool group and your email address list, you have a gold mine of information and expertise. I would never have the skill or patience to choose the right ob-gyn, so I simply asked friends. Same for the pediatrician, the hairdresser, and the ear piercer. Looking for a piano teacher? Text your buddy with the music degree and ask for a recommendation. Need a good eyebrow threader? Ask the next person you see with awesome arches.

Systemize. Stop reinventing the wheel and commit to creating only the wheels that absolutely need inventing. The more simple systems you have in place, the less you will have to use the decision-making part of your brain. Plan your menus, organize your wardrobe, and have a consistent date night with your spouse set in stone, along with a pre-booked babysitter. Make a list of the restaurants you want to go to and tick them off one by one. The fewer decisions you need to make, the better.

Break Things Down, One Bite at a Time. Sometimes we delay decision making, thinking that clarity will come knocking on our door later, tomorrow, or next week. That is an absolute lie to yourself. Maybe you are having trouble with a decision because there are too many steps involved. If choosing a summer vacation destination is too daunting, then break it down into little steps. First, talk to your family about the kind of vacation you'd like to go on. Mountains or beach? City or country? Active or relaxing? Then think about your budget and the geographical area you'd like to target. If you break a decision down into smaller steps, each individual step will be a whole lot less daunting.

SETTING UP YOUR MOM CAVE

What does your wife do all day? She takes care of

your world; give her the respect she deserves.

—DR. LAURA SCHLESSINGER

While you are streamlining the spaces around you, it is important that you also carve out a space for yourself. The Man Cave has become part of our vernacular, but what about the Mom Cave? Virginia Woolf was right when she said that a woman needs "a room of her own." You may not have an entire room to spare, but depending on your budget, you can create a simple niche with your laptop, your planner, and a comfortable chair. Managing the world of your family requires a clear spot for clear thinking.

Whatever the size of your Mom Cave, make sure that you are surrounded by items that make you smile and that everything within your cave is easily accessible.

The Mom Cave is like your control room, where you have all the family's comings and goings clearly organized. To give you an idea of what it can look like, here is a guided tour of the key items in my very own Mom Cave. Each of us is at a different stage in our family life, and each mom in your car-pool group will set up her Mom Cave differently, so start off simple and add and delete as necessary.

1. Information Central (a magnetic board where invitations, appointments, and school notices are posted).

2. A digital filing cabinet, connected to the scanner, for easy storage and retrieval of those precious documents.

3. Labeled bins for each child. This is where I put items that don't fit into regular categories (such as stickers to hide from younger sister, new pretty Band-Aids hidden from view until the next boo-boo, or a reading book bought on sale and ready to give to Junior next month).

4. Assorted colored magazine files for each child's papers that will go into long-term storage.

5. Communication shelf, which holds checkbooks, envelopes, stamps, and stationery.

6. Computer with Google calendar, where all appointments are noted and synced regularly with my phone.

7. Receipt-collection box. Mine is a repurposed record album storage box. Each day, all receipts go into this box (my husband puts them here too), so at the end of the year, when tax time rolls around, they are all in one place, ready to be sorted out.

Aside from my permanent Mom Cave at home, I also have a mobile Mom Cave. If I know I am going to have a forty-five-minute chunk of time alone between appointments, I will leverage that time, rather than waltzing into the local Target and ending up in the Pringles section. I have a bag with my laptop, my charger, my planner pad, and a phone charger, and I am good to set up shop anywhere with a wi-fi connection. In fact, a substantial portion of this book was written at the Key Biscayne Starbucks!

FILING SYSTEM RULES

There are some basic rules that apply to any filing system, whether it is an old-fashioned paper filing system in a metal cabinet or a shiny new digital scan-and-file system.

- It's all about retrieval. File according to how you will think about finding it. Don't file your new license plate information under "automobile" if you will be looking under "car" two months from now.
- Keep vital information in a handy place, and take the time to keep the vital documents highly current. You never know what forms you will need *now*.
- Set fixed times each week to file or scan.
- If you have a digital system, back it up with both online backup and physical backup.
- If you have a paper system, once a year go through your filing cabinet and prune outdated or unnecessary papers.

PART II

THE SYSTEM IS THE

SOLUTION

SYSTEMIZED LIVING

THE SIMPLE WAY TO MAKE TIME
FOR WHAT MATTERS

The system is the solution.

— AT&T

Fifteen minutes can save you
15 percent or more.

— GEICO

THE idea behind systemized living is to have a silent but powerful set of systems and support that gets things done without your direct involvement. Systemizing allows you to leverage your time and minimize needless thinking and planning, so you can do the things you choose to do smarter and in the best way you can.

Systemizing takes patience, trust, and a healthy portion of attention to detail, but in no time you will be living a much calmer life and will see the beauty in no longer having to reinvent the wheel.

And the good news is that this isn't a new concept for you. You already have at least a few simple systems in place; otherwise you would be out buying a new toothbrush every morning, calling the locksmith to make new house keys for you every evening, and never having salt on your fries. All you have to do is take the systems you already have in place and apply the same logic to other areas of your life. You wouldn't use a new toothbrush every day, so why would you do your laundry differently every week or approach your car-pool schedule fresh every Monday morning?

WHY YOU NEED TO SYSTEMIZE

Simply put, you need to systemize so you don't have to think. Obviously, you have to think about some things; you're required to use your brain every day. But there is no reason you should have to decide each day at 6:00 p.m. what to make for dinner that night, or think about where to put the toys and papers that are all over the living room floor, or wonder what to pack in the kids' lunch boxes ten minutes before the bus comes.

To the extent that it is possible, don't make so many decisions. Do what you can to automate your life.

—DR. MEHMET OZ

Instead of trying to figure these things out every day, when you are tired and the kids are running around in circles singing holiday tunes at the top of their lungs, make the decision just once, or

YOU NEED TO

SYSTEMIZE

SO YOU DON'T HAVE TO

just once a week. If you have a rock-solid organization system for toys, books, clothes, kitchen utensils, whatever, you don't have to think when you are putting them away. If you have a good meal-planning system, then once a week you'll need to sit down and use your brain to plan out the week. But after that, all you need to do is look at the chart on the fridge and the answer will be right there. Not having to think too hard about these everyday things will free up your brain cells to focus on more important, more interesting, more fun things.

Basically, you need to think like a CEO. You are the CEO of your family and your home, and your "company" needs certain systems in place to flow smoothly. Just as the CEO of Federal Express wants to see all the FedEx jets flying efficiently around the world and all the packages delivered on time, you want to sit back and watch the constantly smart and efficient motion of your life. And if you realize that the planes not being refueled the night before results in consistent delays in their morning departures and packages arriving late each day, you will want to tweak that system. Being organized and ahead of the game will directly correspond to how many systems you do and do not have working in your life.

Essentially, your home should run as seamlessly as a corporation, involving many simple yet sturdy systems.

Also, while we're on the basics of systemizing, I want to emphasize that your past is not your potential, and it is *never* too late to systemize your life and become calmer and more focused on what matters more. Just because you have been really bad about your laundry, bedtimes, or flossing (or all of the above), do not think that you can't change. Maybe your inner cynic is right and learning about meal plans when your toddler was three months old would have saved you months of baby blues, but that doesn't mean that the time isn't right now as well. Plod on regardless.

*The best time to plant a tree was
twenty years ago. The next best time is now.*

—CHINESE PROVERB

EXPONENTIAL GAINS: WHERE PROJECTS MANAGE THEMSELVES, AND THEN SOME

The greatest force in the world? Compound Interest.

—ALBERT EINSTEIN

Another argument for systemization—and I think one of the strongest—is the beauty and elegance of exponential gains. Exponential growth is the magic behind such momentum-building theories as successful retirement funds, dubious pyramid schemes, and the scuzzy mold in your shower. Exponential growth is what happens once key ingredients are set in place and then gather crucial momentum entirely on their own, without you lifting a finger.

Let's take a moment and compare linear and exponential growth. Without putting an exponential spin on things, you are left with linear growth; you are adding instead of multiplying. Linear growth is defined as growth that is predictable and always the same, such as footsteps, your age, or the dates on your calendar. Each component of linear growth is in business for itself, with no collaboration or group power.

Exponential growth, by contrast, may require an initial investment, but then there is the magic of the snowball effect, in which the project itself gains momentum without relying on you to keep that momentum going. Visualize being at the top of a snowy hill where a competition is being held for the largest snowball at the base of the hill. You could either roll a snowball down the hill, letting it gain momentum and become as large as a house, or you could stuff it in your pocket and carry it down the hill. Yes, this is actually the *literal* snowball effect, but you get the point. With 5 + 5 + 5, you have 15, but with 5 x 5 x 5, you're way ahead at 125.

How do you bring the gains of exponential living into your life? Ask yourself this question at regular intervals: *What can be working while I am not?* In a very simple form, which probably already applies to your life, linear growth is buying one box of mac and cheese every few days, while exponential growth is buying ten boxes and storing them in the pantry; that saves you having to think about buying more for the next two months. Ovens, dishwashers, slow cookers, washing machines, and a host of other fabulous machines can be preset to cook, clean, heat, and wash your world while you are doing other things. With a constant stream of only linear tasks, you get closer while never quite succeeding. You can't get ahead if you buy only one item each time you go to the store. And you can't get ahead if you are doing absolutely everything by yourself, one task at a time.

SYSTEMS ≠ BORING

If you are experiencing some anxiety as you contemplate a drab, assembly-line world of systems that take all the creativity and color out of your life, know that you are in good company. Many of us feel an initial resistance to creating systems, worrying that we will get stuck in a mindless rut. And yes, that might be true if it applied

SYSTEMS ≠ BORING*

*SYSTEMS DON'T MAKE
YOU BORING, THEY
MAKE YOU SMART

to playtime with your kids or your favorite hobby. But for most daily tasks, systems work beautifully.

Systems do not make you boring; they make you smart. Think back to the time when you finally cracked the code on that perfect chocolate cake or when you finally worked out how to get your baby to sleep. Once he slept through the night, did you then decide to experiment with different routines each night, to see if they would work as well? Or did you shout "Hallelujah!" and stick to the system that allowed you uninterrupted sleep? The beauty of all the systems you already have working in your life (and yes, you already have some) is that you have discarded what does not work in favor of what does. You have figured out what works for you and you have chosen to stop reinventing the wheel.

The beauty of incorporating more of these systems into your life for the day-to-day stuff is that it will free you up to use your mind however you want, without being dragged down by the tyranny of constantly having to reinvent the wheel. Think of yourself as Michelangelo, whose hands are finally free to paint after months of holding paint pots.

SYSTEMIZING YOUR APPROACH TO LIFE: TIME MANAGEMENT TIPS FOR WORKING SMARTER

In the pages that follow, I am going to give you ideas and advice for systemizing both the way you organize your home and the way you perform different tasks. And as you are going about creating these systems, I want you to also look at how you use your time in general. Ironically, even though time is what we all need more of, it is also what we tend to waste the most. The following basic time management tips will help you systemize your approach to life, allowing you to do things more intelligently and more effectively, even if they are not part of a specific system.

※

The key is in not spending time, but in investing it.

— STEPHEN COVEY

Plan Ahead. One skill I cannot emphasize enough is planning ahead. I call it *getting ahead of now*. This basically means that you need to get ahead of living in the present by constantly thinking "What can I do now that will make things easier later on?" It is the organic, low-fat, yet delicious breakfast of champions, because you aren't actually doing *more* work, you are just doing it ahead of time and making things simpler. Think of the areas in your life that tend to give you the most stress, and think of how you can work things out to be taken care of earlier, or at least how you can get the task started, even if you can't quite finish it. By choosing to take care of things earlier, you are choosing to lower your stress level.

Join the 5:00 a.m. Club. Could you possibly go to sleep earlier and join the 5:00 a.m. Club ? Getting ahead while most of the world is still asleep yields tangible benefits. This works particularly well when you also include an afternoon power nap, but it works particularly badly if you skip that nap and your daughter needs a lot of help and patience with a science project that evening. Be strategic. It is not a win-win if you are an ogre by 4:00 p.m.

Block Out Chunks of Time. Have you ever noticed how "later" quite often means "never"? Are you still planning to put baby photos in an album "later," even though your son just started high school? If something needs to get done, give it a time slot for that week. Set your timer for an amount of time you can tolerate, and get to work. When the time is over, mark the task as done, or assign the remaining part to a time slot for the following week. Don't think of the thirty minutes you blocked off to rearrange your toy cabinets as overwhelming; think of it as a chocolate bar and take care of it one thirty-minute chunk at a time.

·͟ᴛ͟·

The bad news is that time flies;
the good news is that you are the pilot.
—MICHAEL ALTSHULER

Batch Tasks Together. The last time you went grocery shopping, I hope you put more than one item in your cart. If you did, then you began your formal education in batching. You needed forty-five different items, and since you had already taken the time to drive to the store and were walking around with the cart anyway, it made sense to buy more than one item at a time. The same logic applies to performing certain tasks. Boring or routine tasks can create procrastination and anxiety. One good way to get these things done quickly is to batch them. This means that you do them all in a row, just like the grocery shopping. You will be able to do them more quickly, because there is less "start-up time" and more time to fully concentrate than if you had spread them out.

TOP TASKS TO START
BATCHING IMMEDIATELY

- Returning phone calls
- Replying to emails
- Filing
- Bill paying

SUNDAY IS YOUR FRIEND

People often say that Sunday is their least favorite, most stressful day of the week. The weekend is almost over, and school and work start again the next day. In my house, Sunday is the day when I block out time and truly get ahead for the week, making plans and getting things done before the manic stress of the school week and workweek begins to overwhelm my family. For your family, this moment may be on a different day of the week. Whenever it is, pick a time during the week that you will use to get ahead.

Children
- Together with your child, pick out clothes and hair accessories for the week.
- Organize your children's bedrooms and show them the huge difference that fifteen focused minutes can make.
- Clean out backpacks.
- Help your children plan their week visually, and discuss any supplies they might need.
- Plan your Sunday backward so that the kids can have an early night before another hectic week.

Mom
- Pick out your clothes for the week.
- Plan your week in your planner pad.
- Clean out the car.
- Go through all the mail that has piled up during the week.

Kitchen
- Plan meals for the week.
- Buy ingredients for school lunches and dinners for the week.
- Buy snack items for the children for the week.
- Pack up snacks for the week.

THE EVOLUTION OF A SYSTEM

Whether you are reorganizing your cutlery drawer, reconfiguring your car-pool schedule, or revamping your current laundry routine, the creation of a system will follow some basic steps.

The first thing you need to do is to figure out *what* needs to be systemized. This is sort of a "pre-step" to the systemization process. Start by selecting *one area* to work on. I know it is tempting to start multiple projects at the same time, but trust me, it doesn't work.

Ask yourself: What is not working? There is probably a major area that will jump out at you. Use the 80/20 rule and choose the area that is causing you the most conflict in your home, or the one that is making you feel super guilty, or the one that is causing the most anxiety.

You want to make sure you take care of one item all the way through and make sure it is being sustained before you work on the next item. That doesn't mean you'll take care of just one thing a week or a month—it doesn't have to take a long time to create and implement systems.

As you create each system, ask yourself four questions:

1. What Is Your Vision?

The first step in developing your perfect laundry, mealtime, closet, or whatever plan is determining your vision for a smoothly running system. What would make you smile when you think about laundry, mealtime, closets, or whatever? I call this "the shoulder test." What would make your tense shoulders relax? And don't be afraid to think outside the box. Your vision does not have to be the same as your mother's or your sister's or your perfect neighbor's. Everyone is different, and everyone should do things her own way. And remember, if you really, really hate doing something, there are many options for outsourcing and doing things differently.

2. How Can You Achieve That Vision?

The next step is figuring out how to make your goal a reality. This is where you actually develop the specific system. Each system needs to include the *what*, the *how*, and the *when*. For example, if you are designing a laundry system, you need to figure out what you are going to focus on (towels and sheets, kids' clothes, parents' clothes), how you are going to sort it, and when you are going to wash each type of clothing. If you are planning mealtimes, you need to figure out what you want to plan (just dinners, all three meals, just weekdays, every day), how you are going to make that plan (consult recipe books, make lists of go-to meals, write the menu on a chalkboard in the kitchen), and when you are going to do it (when to make the weekly plan, when to do the shopping). While you are doing this, make sure you are really focused on making the system as simple as you possibly can. That will increase its likelihood of lasting beyond next Tuesday.

3. How Can You Remember the System?

Compared to step 2, this step is a breeze. You just need to transfer your system out of your brain and keep it visible somewhere. This is the opposite of "out of sight, out of mind." You want your system in sight and in mind. This is where digital calendars and even paper and pen come in handy. Think of the best way to remind yourself and the family of the new system, such as a schedule posted above the washing machine, a meal chart on the fridge, a system of labels for toy bins, or anything else you can think of.

4. How Can You Keep the System Alive?

Once the system is all in place and flowing, you might be tempted to let things slide when something more exciting comes along to distract you. Laundry systems might fall apart when guests come in from out of town. That's fine if the time lapse is a day or two, but do your best to keep things afloat. Even if it's not exciting or challenging and even feels somewhat boring, keep it going. Remember, it is reducing your stress and maximizing your productivity. And if the system isn't working—because, say, the children are too tired after school or the chart is too complicated—don't shoot down the system; just tweak it.

Your new mantra: Liberation through systemization.

A SYSTEMIZED HOME IS AN ORGANIZED HOME

⊰ 5 ⊱

SYSTEMIZING PLACES & THINGS

A SYSTEMIZED HOME IS AN ORGANIZED HOME

SYSTEMIZING places is very simple: It's all about retrieval. *If you can't find something, then you don't own it.* You are simply doing it a favor by housing it, but it is not useful in any way to you and your world. You've heard the expression "What color is your parachute?" Well, how about "*Where* is your parachute?"

※

More possessions, more worry

—RABBI HILLEL

When committing to a simpler, more "retrievable" home, it is very important not to over-sentimentalize objects. Feel free to create a sentimental box (or two) to keep mementos in, but don't confuse that with living in a sentimental *home*. Who you are comes from the inside, not from the items you have collected in dusty, cluttered corners of your home.

IT'S ALL ABOUT RETRIEVAL: THE "LAWS" OF AN ORGANIZED, SYSTEMIZED HOME

- If you can't find it, then you don't own it.
- Have less in your home.
- Buy less.
- Store like with like.
- Store dislike with dislike (in the garbage).
- Have a "giveaway" bag or box close at hand at all times.
- Create simple, logical systems.

In her book *Organizing from the Inside Out,* Julie Morgenstern introduces the concept of the Kindergarten Organizing System. I believe there is a simple brilliance to this idea. Have you ever noticed how nicely kindergarten teachers organize their class-rooms? Similar items are batched together, containers are labeled, and there is a happy environment with no guessing as to where the markers might be hiding.

This is precisely the system you want to create throughout your home. You want items to be accessible, and you want to be able to clean them up (or, better yet, have your husband or children clean them up) simply and effortlessly. The kindergarten system can work for any area of your house, from homework corners to closets to playrooms. It can also work in any kind of home; you can have the finest mansion in town and still use the kindergarten system, with your granite, marble, and cherrywood fixtures instead of colored plastic bins.

FIVE SIMPLE STEPS TO CREATING A KINDERGARTEN SYSTEM

1. Set aside a block of time.
2. Clear everything out of the space you are focusing on.
3. Assess the space and decide what it would best be used for. Decide whether you have containers you can repurpose or whether you need to buy some.
4. Invite back the items that belong there, put them into the containers, and then label the containers.
5. Repurpose or give away the rest.

Not sure where to begin? Look for piles of clutter around the house and create a kindergarten system right there. Having to remind the children too often to move their shoes from in front of the door? Put a cute wicker basket there to corral the shoes. Got fined last month for an overdue library book? Designate a container where all library books are put right after reading.

TIP: A CRISIS IS A TERRIBLE THING TO WASTE

A friend of mine once said she finds it easier to work out when she's mad. I feel the same way about organizing. So the next time you get worked up over a parking ticket, a tax hike, or an argument with your boss, don't go straight to the potato chips. Instead, roll up your sleeves and organize something!

CLOSETS: OUT WITH THE SHOULDER PADS, IN WITH THE RELAXED SHOULDERS

An organized closet will save you much more than time. It will allow you to begin and end each day on a note of serenity.

—ELYSZE HELD

(fashion stylist, styleoutofthecity.com)

No matter how big or small a home is, whether it is an apartment or a castle, everyone has unruly closets. Thus, closets are an excellent place to start your systemization process. Although the chaos may be hidden behind closed doors, it is likely weighing on you constantly. So let's create a system for your closets:

1. What Is Your Vision?

With a closet, your vision is probably pretty basic—for example, "I'd like to be able to know where things are and be able to find them when I need them." That means that you need to have a designated spot for each thing in each closet and a way to remember what goes where. Onward to step 2.

2. How Can You Achieve That Vision?

Chances are, you have too many things in your closet. Remember the 80/20 rule? If you look through the clothes in your closet and realize that you really wear only a few items most of the time, don't worry—you are in good company. Give those items prime real estate in your closet, and move some of the less frequently worn things farther back. Better yet, give them away.

Now that you've purged the contents of your closet, it is time to organize what is left. First, make sure you have adequate storage space to put everything away. Investing in good, interchangeable closet systems will yield benefits years later. This doesn't have to be an expensive, customized closet makeover; simple shelving systems and storage bins from Target or IKEA can make a world of difference in your closet

Use logic to decide where each type of clothing should go in the closet. Unless you live in the Arctic tundra, chances are you have seasons. Out-of-season items should be kept out of sight to maximize the space you have left. Each year, when you are rotating your clothes with the new season, make sure you take a hard look at things before you store them away to hibernate until next year. If you didn't wear something this year, are you really going to wear it next year?

3. How Can You Remember the System?

If most of the clothes are visible in your closet, you probably don't need to make labels for each section. Just remember to keep like with like and hang your dresses back up in the dress section, rather than in the pants section. For things that are stored away in containers, such as out-of-season clothes or scarves or even shoes in shoe boxes, make sure that they are labeled clearly, so you can see what they are and find what you need.

4. How Can You Keep the System Alive?

This can sometimes be the hardest part of closet organization. We've all experienced the blissful first few days after we clean out and organize a closet. Each time you open the door, it seems so neat and bright and shiny. But after a few days or weeks, you are in a rush and you just throw the shoes in on the floor, or jam a T-shirt onto the shorts shelf. Remind yourself that the only way to keep the bliss alive is to take the time to put things away where they go. It really only takes an extra ten seconds to put something on a hanger and hang it in the right spot, rather than just tossing it onto a shelf. You may think you are in too much of a rush to afford that extra ten seconds, but unless your child is about to jump off the roof, you probably are not.

Another thing to keep in mind is that you can always rearrange things if the system is not working. After a week, you may realize that it makes sense to keep your work blouses with your work suits rather than with the other blouses, or to put your running bras on the same shelf as your workout clothes rather than with the other underwear. If doing so will make it easier for you to keep the system alive, then by all means move those shirts.

Note: Children's closets present challenges of their own, as kids grow out of clothes and change their tastes with blinding speed. Check my website (www.sobeorganized.com) for specific tips on how to organize children's closets.

CASE STUDY
Ita's Closet: Multiple Wardrobe Personality Disorder

MEET ITA. She has a closet situation (we don't call it a problem) that many of us moms can relate to. In the course of having three children, her weight has changed so often that every time she opens her closet door, she feels like she owns a small consignment shop. The closet has clothes in every size from 6 to 12, with a healthy amount of maternity and nursing items thrown in. Here is how I helped Ita create a system for her closet:

1. What Is Your Vision?
Quite simply, Ita wanted to be able to open her closet door and be able to find clothes that fit her and made her feel good about herself.

2. How Can You Achieve That Vision?
The first thing we did was take everything out of the closet. To really transform the space, we painted the walls a happy color (this is extra credit, and not really required for a basic closet makeover). Ita then made a pile of items, which ended up representing at least half the contents of the closet, to give away to friends, consignment, and charities. The items that survived the purge were invited back into the closet and organized according to type. We created a smaller section with items that she still loved but that were still a little

bit tight. Then we filled and clearly labeled fabric storage bins with freshly laundered maternity and nursing wear, and clothing that was two sizes too small. These bins were stored on the highest shelves.

3. How Can You Remember the System?

Ita labeled each storage bin that was placed up high or out of sight, to be sure that she knew what and where everything was.

4. How Can You Keep the System Alive?

Ita tweaked the system to keep it sustainable. She committed to spending fifteen minutes organizing and housekeeping the closet every Tuesday, so that things did not get out of control. She also purchased a small, pretty bin to keep on the floor of the closet, where she could place things that needed to be put away in storage containers higher up in the closet. When that bin gets full, she gets out the stepladder and puts everything away. Finally, she also discovered a potential flaw in her system that had to be tweaked: Her little girls kept raiding her shoe collection to play dress-up. Simply moving some of the better shoes to a slightly higher shelf solved that dilemma!

KITCHENS: THINK LIKE A RESTAURANT

Our presence in the kitchen seldom resembles the professional chef turned pediatric nutritional expert we once envisioned ourselves becoming. We are often under a time crunch, marinating ourselves in doubt over the vitamin D, protein, and organic vegetables. All in all, preparing meals can be very unpleasant, particularly if there's a teething child around, the milk has gone sour, and you have to have dinner ready in fifteen minutes and can't find the olive oil.

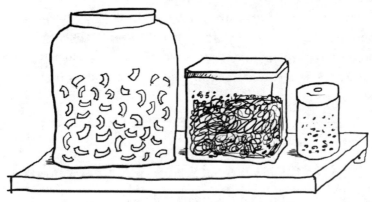

This section will help you figure out how to set up some simple systems in your kitchen, to make it more organized, more efficient, and an overall nicer place to be (though I can't help you with the teething kid).

Once again, let's follow the four steps to systemization:

1. What Is Your Vision?

Your vision is probably pretty simple here. (You will notice as you go through this book that all the visions are relatively simple.) You may want to be able to find what you need, when you need it, in just a few seconds. You may want to be able to prepare meals (or have someone else prepare them) in a pleasant, neat, organized environment. You may want to have a better system for what you store in the kitchen and what you don't.

Whatever your vision, picture it in your head and then write it down somewhere so you can see your goal.

2. How Can You Achieve That Vision?

Despite what the home design magazines say, you don't have to have acres of granite countertops, cherrywood cabinets, and stainless-steel appliances to be organized and successful in the kitchen. Have you ever gone to a restaurant and seen the amazing meals that are put together in a kitchen the size of a shoe box (with not an inch of granite in sight)?

It is really not all about the fairy tale kitchen (though that Viking range wouldn't hurt); it's actually about having all the essential items close at hand and recognizing the importance of using every square inch wisely. Use these tips to help you get your kitchen working for you and to hold you over until you have the time, strength, and resources for a total kitchen makeover.

Location, Location, Location. Yes, the laws of real estate apply just as much in the kitchen as they do on Madison Avenue. Assess the prime real estate locations in your kitchen and make sure you are using your square footage wisely

Top-dollar locations are those that are within easy reach; middle-range areas are the cupboards and drawers that are in awkward or out-of-reach spots; and the super cheap, low-rent district is the area you need a step stool to reach. Figure out which items you use the most, and put them in the best neighborhoods.

Workstations—Put Like with Like. Kitchens do well when they are set up as a bunch of mini workstations. By workstation, I don't necessarily mean a spot on the counter where utensils and supplies are laid out ready to be used at a moment's notice. Rather, I mean that all the tools you need for frequent tasks should be grouped together in one spot, whether it be a single cabinet, a drawer, or even on the countertop.

Whether it is snack making, bread making, dinner making, or waffle making, organize your spaces to facilitate the food preparation that happens with the most frequency. Clearly, the sushi you make twice a year doesn't require its own workstation, but the snacks and lunches you prepare each evening do. Literally stand where you prepare the lunches each night (or the waffles on Sunday morning) and make sure you have the things you need within arm's reach. Move things around, and let the real estate rule save you the legwork.

Depending on your family's needs, you might have any number of workstations at this point in your life, including:

- A hot drink station (far out of reach of little children) with tea, coffee, filters.
- A snack station with nonperishable snacks in transparent containers and Ziploc bags.
- A lunch station, with lunch bags, containers, thermoses, and bags ready to be filled.

- A cookie station kitted out with supplies for basic cookie dough, cookie cutters, and aprons.
- A bottle station with all the tools you need for making up, cleaning, and drying baby bottles.

Many of us have our kitchen set up with half-equipped stations. Check yourself the next time you work on a specific task to see how efficient that particular workstation is.

Put Dislike with Dislike . . . and Get It Out of the Kitchen. Kitchens should be where we prepare nurturing food for our families, not where we hoard clutter. Many of us have items we don't like or don't use in our kitchens. How absurd. Get rid of that clutter right away. Not using the avocado wedger you bought at an exaggerated price when it first came out? Send it to your aunt in Florida, who eats avocados far more frequently. Not using all seven of your heavy iron cake tins? Give some to friends and neighbors who will, and then you'll stand a greater chance of getting a piece of cake when they use them.

Think Before You Bulk. Many of us clog up valuable kitchen space with bulk items, such as eight rolls of paper towels, gigantic canisters of rice, and big bags of snacks. Make sure you use food items frequently enough to warrant storing them in the kitchen, and don't buy so much that it will go stale before you can eat it. For condiments, consider putting some in smaller bottles and refilling them from larger bottles you keep elsewhere. For paper goods, think like a restaurant and keep one or two current items in the kitchen and the rest in a separate storage space.

Bulk Snacks. By all means, buy your snacks in bulk, but be strict about storing the extras up high. Out of sight is really the only way to keep those treats out of your children's minds. For obvious reasons (think back to your childhood), do your best to not let the children know where your bulk-storage hiding places are.

Save Space by Limiting Choices. The paradox of choice works for your reusable plastic containers the same way it works for buying plant fertilizer. I do not want to see one more kitchen drawer stuffed to capacity with a continuum of sizes for every possible food storage need. Assess the needs you actually have, and then pick three or four sizes of containers—and that's it. Stack them together, then set up bins in drawers or cabinets for easy retrieval.

3. How Can You Remember the System?

Because you use your kitchen many times a day, you probably won't need to label all your cupboards and drawers. You will quickly get used to where things go. For bulk food stored in reusable containers in a pantry or closet, it can help to use a label maker to mark the canisters so that you know when you are out of something and need to buy more.

4. How Can You Keep the System Alive?

The only way to keep a well-organized kitchen well organized is to put things away where they belong immediately after using them—and, perhaps more important, to train the rest of your family to do the same. If everything has a designated spot that makes sense and is relatively easy to find, you all should be able to put things where they go. Then when dinner needs to be ready in fifteen minutes, you will know exactly where the olive oil is (but, sorry, the teething kid might still be screaming).

Your kitchen organizational needs will evolve as fast as your children grow. Before you know it, the baby bottle station will be replaced with the preschool snack station and then the school lunches station. Stay on top of your kitchen and your needs from month to month and year to year, and be prepared to do a little redistricting if you need to move things around or create different workstations.

BEDROOMS: WHERE IS THE ACTUAL BED?

Contrary to popular belief, your bedroom is not for hiding piles of clutter from the public. It is your most private, personal space, and your focus should be on keeping it clean, uncluttered, and refreshing, so that you can walk in there and relax, away from the chaos.

1. What Is Your Vision?

Your bedroom should not be an extension of your home office or an annex for your children's toys. Aside from things in your closet, anything that is not directly connected to your rest and relaxation should be given a new home. If you need to keep a bedtime book for your daughter or your newborn's diapers in your room, find a special space for them in your closet.

2. How Can You Achieve That Vision?

Less Is More. Just as in every other area of your life, less is more. The pieces of furniture that support your relaxation and rest are welcome; other things are not. So yes to the relaxing candles and no to the wireless printer. Yes to the neat bookshelf to help store your books, and no to the box you are taking to the post office tomorrow.

Give the Walls a New Coat of Paint. The cheapest and most effective way to change the atmosphere in a room is to change the color of the walls.

BEDROOMS

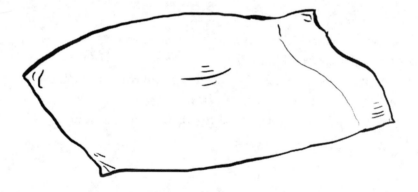

Good Lighting. Your bedroom should ideally have a nice blend of natural daylight from the windows, enough light to be able to see clearly in the closets, and a dimmer switch or night-light to make the room better for sleeping at night.

Window Treatments. Good window treatments should enable you to easily open up the room to natural daylight, darken it when you want to sleep (even if the sun has already come up), and give you the option of privacy. They also give the room a finished look, which is an added bonus.

Tranquil Finishes. Keep an eye out for pretty light switches and decorative hooks to add extra touches of tranquillity to your room. Don't overbuy and fill your room with kitsch, but do keep an eye out for things that will add to the environment of tranquillity and peace.

Create a Smart System for Those Books. If you have already gone digital, then this paragraph is not for you. Go back to your clutter-free iPad or Kindle and send our regards to Hemingway. But for the rest of you avid readers who still haven't come to terms with the idea of giving up an actual paper book, you need a way to organize all those books you are planning to read. I don't want you going to sleep with a Leaning Tower of Pisa made out of books hovering over your head. Remember the kitchen section, where I asked you to think like a restaurant and keep on hand only what you are currently using? Do the same with your books. Keep the bulk of them in a different location, and pick out just a few books or magazines that will make it to your night table at a given time. Consider organizing the others in different categories, such as library books, books to return to friends, work-related books, etc., to enable you to pass them on more efficiently.

Make Your Bed Every Day. For Real. Your mother was right. Respecting your need for an organized, clear environment sets the tone for your day. Besides, it will make you feel human again when you walk back into your room in the evening.

Organize Your Clothing-Management Systems. Everything in your bedroom should be organized in its own mini system. The key areas that most people need to address relate to clothing; they include dry cleaning, laundry, and items that need hand-washing or repairing. On my website (www.sobeorganized.com), I provide much more information on how to get on top of these systems.

TRICKS FOR KEEPING YOUR CHILD'S ROOM FANTASTIC

Question Big Items. Before your child receives, for a birthday or a prize, an item that is going to take up a lot of space, ask yourself whether this is a wise move. If it is going to look too large or attract clutter, you may want to help guide your child toward picking something else.

Real Estate Value. From time to time, reevaluate the real estate value of the items in your kids' rooms. If they are currently going through the Barbie phase, then you may want to set up easily accessible containers near the dollhouse and move other things to less accessible spots. Ditto for the rollerblading phase and the stuffed animal phase.

An Ounce of Prevention. On as many evenings as possible, the children should set a timer and straighten up their rooms for five minutes. Make it a game before they brush their teeth. Then they should chose a fixed time each week—for instance, on the weekend—to do a deeper, fifteen-minute cleanup of their toys and clothes. Parents should not micromanage these cleanups; the goal is for the children to internalize that it's their responsibility to manage their possessions.

Shoes. First, you know that you have too many pairs of shoes. Don't even try to deny it. Prune them down to the essentials and give away the rest. Now that you can actually fit all your shoes into your closet, make sure that your shoe storage system is as user friendly as it is functional. Then the trick is to commit to putting your shoes away in their little homes, rather than leaving them lying around your otherwise tranquil room.

3. How Can You Remember the System?

Be brutal about not letting clutter pile up in your bedroom by having a fixed morning schedule and a fixed time each week for cleanup.

4. How Can You Keep the System Alive?

Be on the lookout for new organizing items you might need in your room. If you see clutter starting to pile up, determine what you need to keep the bedroom organized and relaxed—maybe a new jewelry box or a better shoe storage system. Everything from your jewelry to your reading material should be kept in an organized manner.

THE GIFT DRAWER

Reduce last-minute stress by maintaining a small gift drawer, box, or shelf. For instance, keep some pretty tea towels around; they are super light and can be thrown into a suitcase when someone in your family is staying with an out-of-town friend. Keep a male and female baby gift and nice stationery, candles, or a key chain for last-minute gifts. When you have a gift drawer filled with the essentials, you are less likely to waste an hour running around looking for gifts, paying top dollar and losing your cool. Additionally, have gift bags and tissue on hand for simple gift wrapping that doesn't take up valuable space.

CHILDREN'S PLAYROOMS: TAMING THE TIDE OF TOYS

Tell me and I forget. Teach me and I remember.

Involve me and I learn.

—BENJAMIN FRANKLIN

Even if your house doesn't have a separate playroom, don't skip this section. All kids have a place where the majority of their toys reside and most of their playing takes place, whether it is a family room, their bedroom, or smack in the middle of your formal living room. Use this section to organize that part of your home.

A child's play area should be a nurturing and creative environment. You want your children to feel safe and inspired as they create Lego masterpieces or launch their first paper airplane.

1. What Is Your Vision?

The vision is twofold. First, you need a special place for the children to learn and grow. Second, you need to have a home where you aren't at risk of herniating a disk by tripping over Mr. Potato Head and the rest of his potato family.

2. How Can You Achieve That Vision?

Control Clutter. It's hard for any of us to be organized when we have too much stuff. Before the next birthday, over the summer break, or before the holidays, encourage children to give away some of their stuff to make the organizing and containerizing manageable. I never advocate giving away items that are very important to your child; however, the majority of children today have too much stuff and not enough space or even time to play with it all, let alone organize it neatly. If your children can learn to view their possessions as *fluid* and likely to bring joy to other people when they don't need them anymore, then you have earned a special place in your future son- or daughter-in-law's heart.

Give Everything a Home. Once you have less "stuff," organize it in a rock-solid system. There are dozens of toy organizers out there, from the simple and inexpensive to the elaborate and costly. Choose the system that works for your time and budget and give everything its own place. For younger children, label every bin or cubby with words or pictures. Every toy with little pieces should get its own container, and containers with small pieces should be kept up high if you have younger children.

Once you have the system in place, go over it with your children (or, better yet, create it together). After the kids have learned the system, they have the choice of putting their things away in the right place or not. Then you, as the parent, have the choice of whether you are going to create a consequence if things are not put away in the right place, whether you are going to let things slide, or something in between. Personally, I like the idea of the consequence box, where items that are not put away are confiscated by invisible police and then have to be redeemed for chores or some other parent-pleasing action. That works great if the parent is super motivated, the children are somewhat gullible, and the parent can be consistent. I used it for my first two children but then was too tired and outnumbered to be consistent with the younger kids. Whatever you do, be consistent. Maybe you can create a cleanup game that you play together.

ONE IN

ONE OUT

One In, One Out. Children should also begin to learn that it isn't necessary, or even desirable, to have an infinite number of things. Teach them to pay attention to the number of toys, scrapbook supplies, hair things, or whatever that they have, and encourage them to commit to passing on older items when new ones come their way. This practice, once encouraged, will begin to flow naturally most of the time—except for once in a while when the scrapbook supplies are shiny and glittery and your daughter cannot for the life of her decide which sticker pack to give away. (*Note:* This can also backfire, when your child wears her expensive new shoes twice and then decides they are actually too tight or too uncomfortable and tells you lovingly that she wants to share them with other children.)

3. How Can You Remember the System?

Keep the system and the rules posted in a visible place, and consider putting them in photo or picture format for younger children.

4. How Can You Keep the System Alive?

Review the system regularly to make sure it is working. If there is one particular toy that is always lying around, maybe you need to make its home more accessible. Keep working at it, and involving your children, until you find the system that works for you.

Make sure to reinforce your kids when the system works. Children might initially be quite resistant to the idea that they are being remotely organized. So "catch" your children doing organized things and comment with specific praise. Instead of global praise ("Wow! You're so organized!"), use specific comments ("You put your bag by the front door—now that's organized!" or "Markers back in the right bin—nice work"). No need to break out the pom-poms, but you get what I mean.

CASE STUDY
Jody, the Budding Artist

JODY recently turned four and has become smitten with any-thing to do with coloring, markers, crayons, and stickers. After years of corralling the trucks and action figures of Jody's three older brothers, her mom, Lisa, was unprepared for the ava-lanche of art supplies left strewn all over her playroom.

1. What Is Your Vision?

Let's face it: Down the road, we want our children to be orga-nized and know how to manage their time and space. Lisa came to me asking if it was possible to instill these values in an art-crazed, marker-wielding pipsqueak.

2. How Can You Achieve That Vision?

First, we rearranged the playroom as a decent imitation of a Montessori classroom. With art supplies stored in individual designated bins, we made cleanup as easy and obvious as possible. Items that were used really often were given high priority on the real estate scale, and we took the tops off those bins to enable easy cleanup. Then it was a question of teach-ing Jody to put the art supplies back after she used them.

3. How Can You Remember the System?

We labeled each bin with a picture of the particular art sup-ply it contained, so Jody and Lisa could easily find what they were looking for.

4. How Can You Keep the System Alive?

Lisa committed to put in a twenty-minute maintenance ses-sion once a week and plugged that into her calendar. That way, any storage containers that could be used more effi-ciently could be reassessed. This session was more effective done away from little Jody's beady eyes.

BATHROOMS: WASHING CLUTTER DOWN THE DRAIN

Our bathrooms are magnets for clutter. With the amount of self-care and beauty products we use today, it is a widespread problem that is as logical to solve as it is frustrating.

1. What Is Your Vision?

Bathrooms should resemble mini spas rather than mini hurricane zones. If you will commit to having less, designating space, and brutally maintaining it, your bathroom can help you achieve the inner tranquillity you strive for.

2. How Can You Achieve That Vision?

Here's the secret: Cull 75 percent of the stuff and brutally organize the other 25 percent. Bingo.

Take It All Out. Take out *e-v-e-r-y-t-h-i-n-g*. Once you have a nice clear space and can hear your own echo, you know you are in a good starting place.

Separate It All. Keep the stuff you *love*, keep a few extras of those beloved things, and give away the rest. Take sample-size items and put them away for the next time you travel, or put them in your guest room.

Designate the Spaces. Remember the real estate rules we spoke about in other sections? They apply even more in a small place like a bathroom. Determine which items you use the most, because if they

BATHROOMS

are not organized properly, then they will be your prime suspects for future clutter offenses.

Think Outside the Box—Literally. Reposition items with an eye for keeping the bathroom streamlined. Consider opening up more hidden space by using your medicine cabinet for things other than medicine, and keep your medicines elsewhere (high up, away from little fingers).

Makeup Madness. No lecture needed: You know you have too much makeup. After getting rid of the expired items, put the items you use daily in an easily accessible spot.

Simplify. Keep checking that the items in your bathroom are being stored in the most effective and simple way, and be on the lookout for even simpler ways for your family to keep organized.

Counter Space. Think of the counter space in your bathroom the same way you think about your driveway—no parking junk! Invest in pretty and functional open-storage containers and have zero tolerance for new clutter.

Shower Yourself with Love, Not with Clutter. Reassess your shower and your shower caddy. Commit to keeping the items you need and use organized, and don't keep extras in the shower. Some of our most lucid thoughts come to us in the shower, and we wouldn't want that bulk-size double pack of shampoo to cloud our new multimillion-dollar idea now, would we?

Think Like a Restaurant. Keep out only what you need for the week, and refill on a weekly basis.

Throw in the Towel on Inefficient Towel Storage. Most bathrooms have ample hanging storage for fresh towels but seldom have an easily accessible *and functional* system for towels that still have a couple more uses in them before they're washed. Create hooks for each family member to have a place to hang towels; there are some really pretty ones out there. If you are short on space, use the back of the door.

3. How Can You Remember the System?

Think of clutter as a six-inch dragonfly flying around your bathroom. You don't have to scream like a crazy woman, but you can't ignore it and hope it will go away of its own accord. Immediately remove any offenders and be vigilant for new ones as they threaten. Have a calendar note to check the system every week or two, and before you buy new toiletries, ask yourself where they are going to be stored.

4. How Can You Keep the System Alive?

Adopt an attitude of zero tolerance for clutter in your relaxation zone.

CASE STUDY
The Boys in the Bathroom

JENNA'S two boys share a bathroom that is light deprived, old-fashioned, and lowest on the totem pole for any remodeling love in their house. The bathroom is cluttered, dysfunctional, and not very much fun to use.

1. What Is Your Vision?
Jenna wanted a low-budget organizational makeover for the bathroom, so Benjamin and Rafi could use it in a clean and efficient manner.

2. How Can You Achieve That Vision?

This bathroom was tiny. There wasn't even room to put in a slim organizer to give the boys some drawer space. We took everything out and kept fewer than a quarter of the items. We then maximized every square millimeter we could find. There was a closet right next to the bathroom that was being used mainly as a communal laundry hamper, and the upper shelves held light bulbs. Recognizing an organizational gold mine sitting right on our doorstep, we created a new laundry system with hampers in each room and got rid of the basket in the closet. The closet had built-in capability for a total of five shelves, and we were able to expand the depth of the current shelves by 40 percent. Armed with this flush new closet, we filled it with tissues, toilet paper, soap, shampoo, and towels. Then we were left with creating a very lean but functional bathroom. We got the boys matching towels with their names on them and put hooks on the back of the door for the towels to dry. We emptied the medicine cabinet of its junk, divided the four shelves, and labeled them with only the boys' names. The toothbrushes, toothpastes, floss, and face wash were all put back in their rightful places.

3. How Can You Remember the System?

We made sure the boys understood where things went and which things belonged in the bathroom and which belonged in the hall closet.

4. How Can You Keep the System Alive?

The bathroom gets deep-cleaned once a week, and towels are replaced. Toilet paper, tissues, soap, and shampoo are replenished as necessary. When cousins or friends sleep over, it gets a little messy, but as long as things are reorganized right after guests leave, the system stays afloat.

LAUNDRY/UTILITY ROOMS: LET'S NOT BLAME THE DRYER FOR THE LOST SOCKS

All too often, a room that serves as a laundry room or a utility room ends up being used as a dumping ground for items that don't have a room of their own. While there is nothing illegal about parking a set of golf clubs in an unobtrusive corner of a laundry room, there is something very wrong about a set of four spare kitchen chairs taking up the bulk of the space in the room and nearly blocking the washing machine.

1. What Is Your Vision?

Keep your cans in your can closet and your linen in your linen closet. Likewise, let your laundry room be a place where the laundry gets done efficiently and even pleasantly.

2. How Can You Achieve That Vision?

Designate the Space. Get rid of the items that don't belong there, and reclaim the space for its original purpose.

Make It Über-Functional. Rather than just plodding on regardless of the roadblocks in your way, take a good look at your space and see if it can be made even more functional. Can you make it any easier on yourself and those using the room? Can you install hangers, shelving, hooks, or rods to make things simpler? Take a look at your favorite organizational catalogs for inspiration.

Put the "Fun" into Functional. If the dingy walls make you want to procrastinate on doing your laundry, then consider painting the walls (or even just one of them) your favorite color to encourage you to use the room more frequently.

LAUNDRY

ROOMS

Small Changes Can Make a Difference Too. Sometimes we have a tendency to think that if we can't redo an entire room, then we will just "make do" until the time is right. Forget that. You might be waiting for a laundry room overhaul for the next thirteen years, and that's a lot of energy you'll be wasting on procrastinating on all that laundry. Bite the bullet and ask yourself what one change could make a difference. Stop sulking; it doesn't suit you.

3. How Can You Remember the System?

Once your laundry or utility room is working in a more efficient manner, use the time you're saving to keep it that way. Consider a weekly deep clean or a daily "clean as you go" to keep things flowing smoothly.

4. How Can You Keep the System Alive?

Like any good system, this room's will need a certain amount of tweaking to keep it afloat. There will be times when your daughter is working on a project that has to be kept in the laundry room for two weeks until it is completed or when your children are unpacking from camp and the sheer smell of their items requires their duffel bags to be quarantined in the laundry room.

CASE STUDY
Jill's Laundry Room: Creating a No-Dumping Zone

JILL had a large laundry/utility room that was such a dumping zone for anything and everything that she didn't even have space to store the five containers of laundry detergent she had bought in bulk.

1. What Is Your Vision?

Jill had to get rid of the illegal space invaders. She needed to designate areas to create mini working zones and open up the space for the right things, so that she could save money by buying in bulk and save her time and her sanity by not tripping over garage-sale fodder on her way to the dryer.

2. How Can You Achieve That Vision?

Jill's first task was to get the broken bicycles and skateboards out of her laundry room. Ditto the old barbecue grill and the old mops. Ditto those horrific dried flowers that should never have been bought in the first place. Next Jill took the time to freshen up the space. She put some rubber mats on the floor and painted the walls bright orange. She knew that a spruce-up doesn't necessarily have to be expensive to be effective.

Next came the fun part. We took out blue tape, and Jill went around designating spaces. She created a laundry zone, a mudroom zone, and an area for a stacker shelf for whole-sale supplies. She then made sure that only items that directly related to those designated spaces were placed in those zones. The next trick was to maximize the use of space within each zone. Jill took a good look at how she could make her designated spots more efficient. For her laundry area, she installed deeper wire shelving above the washer and dryer to enable her to buy more laundry detergent on sale. She also created space for individual laundry baskets for each of her children and an area to hang her shirts to drip-dry, as opposed to hanging them over the washing machine and dryer to dry.

3. How Can You Remember the System?

Creating a more organized laundry room was such a liberating experience for Jill that the only prompting she needed to remember the system was a huge sign that read "No dumping."

4. How Can You Keep the System Alive?

Jill put a note in her calendar on the first of every month to check the laundry room and make sure that the systems she created were still running smoothly. She also made sure that no one cluttered up the space.

GARAGES, BASEMENTS & ATTICS: IT'S REALLY ALL ABOUT RETRIEVAL

Contrary to popular belief, garages, basements, and attics are for storing things so that you will be able to retrieve them, *not* for randomly dumping items in desperation only to never be able to find them ever again.

1. What Is Your Vision?

Simple, but powerful: You want to discover the tremendous time-saving, psychological, and financial benefits of creating orderly garages, basements, and attics by creating a space that enables you to find what you need, when you need it.

2. How Can You Achieve That Vision?

In a perfect world, the government would provide funding and resources for anyone who wanted to organize their garages, basements, and attics. Think of how much happier the country would be if everyone had the pleasure of streamlined spaces to store and organize their belongings. In the interim, here are some tips to help sort out those spaces.

Overhaul—All Hands on Deck. Get some extra hands on board and attack the space. Ask friends and family, or hire a

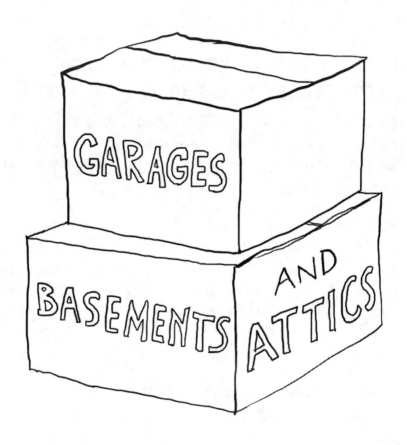

professional organizer. Some jobs are too overwhelming to do alone. The goal is to get rid of as much of the junk as possible and possess the clarity of mind to be able to decide what items really and truly need to be kept. Remember that Pareto's 80/20 rule is alive and well in your garage, basement, or attic, and that a mere 20 percent of the contents are actively being used or will ever be used again.

Stack, Crate, and Label. Once you have corralled the items that are worth keeping, create a simple system to make retrieval easy. Consider using large transparent containers, and label them well. If you can't find that extension cord next Tuesday when your children need it, then you will inevitably experience the frustration of knowing that "it is here, somewhere." Remember, if you can't find it, you don't really own it. So label things well.

3. How Can You Remember the System?

Your cleverly labeled containers will help you find the things you want and guide you as you put other things away for storage in your shiny new organized garage, basement, or attic.

4. How Can You Keep the System Alive?

By the time you have completed the organization of your garage, basement, or attic, you will be so exhausted mentally and physically that you will console yourself with the fact that it was a once-in-a-lifetime experience. Keep it that way by making a diary note to devote an hour or so every month to the upkeep of your organized space.

ENTRYWAYS & MUDROOMS:
PUT YOUR SHOES AWAY

An entryway or mudroom is the focal point of anyone walking into your home, and that includes you and your family. Make it about walking proudly into your lovely home, rather than climbing over mounds of clutter just to get past the front mat.

1. What Is Your Vision?

You are looking for a streamlined welcome area that has a personal and orderly feel, yet also allows the person entering to relax.

2. How Can You Achieve That Vision?

Keys. Most people lose their keys around the home at least once a week (some of us a lot more often than that!). The people who never run around frantically searching for their keys seconds before they need to leave the house are those who put them in the same place every time they come home. Create a place where you will put your keys every time you walk into the house. It can be a pretty plate or a special hook, or they can go right back into your bag. But make a choice and stick to it every time you walk in. You may feel boring, but the freedom you will experience after not losing your keys once over the entire week will make up for it.

Cubbies. Having cubbies is a great way to corral the belongings of young children. Between the backpacks, the shoes, and the extra items needed every other day, a cubby can be a great holding place until the next morning. Depending on space and design constraints, there are a variety of ways to create cubbies. You can go for the standard Pottery Barn–style wooden cubby or use different-colored plastic milk crates or any other such container. The key is that they should be different colors for different children and that

ENTRYWAYS

AND
MUDROOMS

they should not have a lid. Believe it or not, opening a lid is an extra step that can be a huge factor in keeping an area tidy.

Coat Closet. You will need a coat closet or hanging area to keep your entryway or mudroom looking uncluttered. Keep your coat closet organized and current by changing what gets the prime real estate each season. Maximize your vertical space for off-season storage.

Rainy-Day Area. You also need the ability to pull out rain gear with great efficiency when you are late to school and it suddenly starts raining. Rain boots, raincoats, and umbrellas should be accessible within seconds.

Mail. Don't dump the mail on the nearest available surface as you walk in the front door. Assign a place for incoming mail and, if possible, a time when you will sort through it. Before you put the mail down, sift through it over a recycling bin and lose 50 percent of it by weight. Consider having a "to shred" pile also, for sensitive information like credit card offers that are essentially junk mail but that need extra treatment before being trashed.

Table. Depending on the size of your entryway or mudroom, you might have space for a table and mirror. These lend a "homey" feeling to the area. It is also really practical to have a mirror to glance into as you rush out of the house.

Greenery. A fresh plant can add a tranquil touch and do double duty by filtering the air. Note to all of you who profess to have a "black thumb": It really isn't rocket science. You just buy one you like, water it every few days and watch it thrive and enjoy it. Or watch it die and try again.

Clutter. Any clutter that starts to crowd your space in the entryway should, of course, be moved to its actual home (or thrown away). Additionally, you should look for patterns. If a certain item is cluttering your space on a regular basis, then you may want to buy a storage item to corral it. Examples could be a basket for children's shoes or a mail holder that can be affixed to the wall.

3. How Can You Remember the System?

Focus on keeping the area streamlined and tackle the clutter right away. A clutter-free entryway provides a nice, empowering start to your day on your way out and to your evening on your way back in.

4. How Can You Keep the System Alive?

Have zero tolerance for clutter and involve the children in putting their items away in the right spot.

CASE STUDY
Lia's Entryway

LIA'S entryway was a mess, and it bothered her to no end. However, she needed a system that didn't involve constantly screaming at her children, as she was worried that she'd turned into a little too much of a screamer since baby number three was born.

1. What Is Your Vision?

The entryway was a hodgepodge of junk. Lia needed to figure out an easy way to organize everything that belonged there and to get rid of what didn't belong.

2. How Can You Achieve That Vision?

First, Lia moved everything out of the entryway and sorted through it. Things that didn't belong in the area were taken to where they needed to go. She bought a wooden cubby set from Pottery Barn for the children and a magnetic key holder that made it easy to hang her keys up each time she came home. She then bought mini laundry baskets in fun colors and kept one in the car for items that needed to go into the house and one in the entryway for items that needed to go into the car. This allowed her to be in control of any items that were temporarily waiting in the entryway, rather than have them sprawling all over the place. Another huge bonus was that the items from the car could go straight into the more centralized area to be organized, rather than just getting dumped by the front door (again).

3. How Can You Remember the System?

Lia had to embrace her inner security guard and help teach her children the right way to organize their things. It turned out there was no screaming necessary. The children liked the way their items looked in the cubbies and wanted to be like their big cousins who had a similar setup. I also suggested to Lia that she occasionally read an extra book or play an extra game with her kids and tell them that the time saved from not having to clean the entryway had enabled her to spend extra time playing.

4. How Can You Keep the System Alive?

Lia designated Thursday mornings from 10:00 to 10:30 as her time to work on the organization of the entryway. Some weeks, she told me, she didn't actually have anything to do, while other times she said it was a great incentive to get the cubbies organized and cleaned. Basically, she had the situation under control, and she was thrilled.

For more tips on organizing other spaces, such as patios, porches, yards, and even your car, check out my website (www.sobeorganized.com).

CLEANING OUT YOUR PURSE

Carrying around a cluttered bag is a waste of your shoulder muscles and super embarrassing when you have to dump everything out as you try to find a pen. Make cleaning out your bag a ritual, and up the chances of success by attaching it to an existing ritual. Let's say you go to a weekly spinning class: Have a reminder in your calendar to clean out your bag before the class.

SYSTEMIZING DAILY TASKS & ROUTINES

LET YOUR SYSTEMS DO YOUR THINKING

THE following sections offer examples and suggestions for how to systemize your daily tasks and routines, also known as the daily grind. From cleaning to meal planning to laundry to shopping, these are all things that just have to get done. So instead of dreading them and moaning about them, you might as well institute some rock-solid systems to minimize the need to think about these tasks and routines. The less time you spend thinking about what you are *supposed* to do next, the more time you will have for actually doing what you *want* to do next.

HOUSE CLEANING: SYSTEMIZING THAT CLEAN SWEEP

It's not that I don't like order.
I just have a hard time creating it. When I have
a cleaning lady I look to her as God.

— SHERRI MENDEL

The annoying thing about homes is that they don't come with a self-clean button. Whether you do your own cleaning or employ a small army to do it for you, you need to take the time to create and implement a schedule for keeping your home clean.

1. What Is Your Vision?

Cleaning your home really isn't all that complicated when there is a nice juicy system in place. It is only when there is no system, compounded by lots and lots of stuff, that you end up feeling like you'll never see the floor in your house again. By taking the time to leverage as much help as possible and creating a seamless system, you can reduce your cleaning-related stress by about 90 percent. A cleaning service or a desperate call to Mom should take care of the remainder.

2. How Can You Achieve That Vision?

In order to create the right cleaning system for your needs, you should start by asking yourself a few key questions:

Are You Starting with a "Clean Slate"? It is important to note that any cleaning system will work best if you put it in place after you have had a major cleanup. In an ideal world, you would declutter your home, hold a garage sale, and use the proceeds to hire a cleaning crew to whisk through your home, leaving it all sparkly. In the real world, see what you can come up with. Don't start inviting friends and neighbors over to help you; that will turn into a big block party and leave you deeper in the dirt. If the garage sale route is too grand a plan, consider finding someone to watch your children for a few extra hours so you can get some serious cleaning done. Depending on the size of your home and, ahem, the amount of clutter and dirt waiting for your time and attention, it might take you more than one weekend and quite possibly a few evenings in between. Commit to getting it all done within two weeks so your enthusiasm can propel you forward into your new cleaning systems. (Please know, however, that if you don't have the time or the will to do a major cleanup of your home, you can still put some awesome cleaning systems in place. Start with the routine and then de-clutter and deep clean as you go.)

Do You Have Sufficient Cleaning Help? Cleaning help comes in many forms, from hired help to your own two hands to your children and husband. Just like chocolate chip muffins, these all have their pros and cons.

Help from the children: Children need to help around the house for a variety of reasons. First, knowing how to make a basic dinner or how to clean a shower head will help mold them into responsible young adults. Second, it makes them feel like part of a team (because they are), and it is likely to build warm, fuzzy self-esteem and happiness. Third, and perhaps most relevant to this chapter, it helps keep the home running smoothly. Be specific with your kids and write out a simple chore schedule. It will take you seven minutes to write it on the back of an envelope and stick it on the fridge. Add a few smiley faces and thank them. It's really nice when your children help around the house, as opposed to just wrecking the place.

Hired help: Hiring cleaning help is a wise investment if you can afford it, since you are investing in a precious commodity— namely, your sanity. But here's the thing, if you are going to invest the money, please commit to investing the time to make sure that your priorities are made clear to the cleaner. You will need to carve out the time to create as many systems as possible so that your house runs according to the standards and priorities of your unique household. In some homes, the cleanliness of the bathrooms, back yard, or inside of the mailbox is of primary importance, while in other homes it is of no importance whatsoever. In the previous home your cleaner worked in, it may have been paramount that the back patio was swept daily; in your home you may be happy with it being swept weekly. You should be very clear as to what your expectations are, by creating a simple chart with what you would like the cleaner to do whenever he or she comes (daily, weekly, monthly). If appropriate, offer to translate the chart into the preferred language of your cleaner and tweak things as your priorities alter and the seasons change.

Are You Investing In Good Cleaning Products? Remember the last time you were trying to cut an apple with a blunt knife? Frustrating, wasn't it? Like any good artisan, you need the correct tools for the task. I am not saying that until you can afford top-of-the-line cleaning products, you shouldn't clean your home. However, if you invest in a slightly better scrubbing brush, vacuum, or toilet cleaner, then you may find that you get the job done faster and better. Not sure exactly how to clean your fridge? No worries, there is an abundance of "how to" videos on YouTube.

Note: Be sure to put all cleaning products somewhere safe and inaccessible to your small children.

Are You Harnessing Your Best Energy at the Right Times of Day? Another trick to have up your sleeve is tapping into your energy when it is at its best. Some tasks will take a quarter of the time if you do them when your energy level and concentration are at their peak. Of course you are not a robot who can be programmed to an optimal setting, but simply paying attention to how long things take you is definitely worth it. If you are dragging your feet as you try to get something done, consider doing that same task earlier, later, or when you are alone.

CREATING A SIMPLE CLEANING SYSTEM

I wish I had the magic formula that somehow worked for everyone, but when it comes to house cleaning, there is no one-size-fits-all list. You really do need to create a cleaning list for your own home. Keep it super simple and doable, and make tweaks as you see fit. Keep a copy of your cleaning schedule on your computer, so that you never have to reinvent it ever again. Use the following guidelines, but personalize them to your own life. I don't want you cleaning out the dishwasher every two weeks if you never run it and are only using it to store your extensive cookbook collection.

Basically, an effective cleaning system includes the following components, to be done by yourself or outsourced to someone else.

- Daily clean-as-you-go cleaning
- Daily medium-level cleaning
- Weekly deep cleaning
- Monthly or bimonthly deep cleaning
- Annual "spring" cleaning

Daily Clean-as-You-Go Cleaning. To put it bluntly, this is the "don't be such a slob" section. Ouch. I don't mean to offend; I'm just trying to help convey the concept. Without cleaning up after themselves as they go, a family of four can pretty much trash a perfectly orderly home within three hours. Just like your spinning class, it isn't all going to be fun, but the aftereffects will be exhilarating. By choosing to clean up after yourselves as you go, you will save a ton of later cleanup.

The basic premise is to clean up as you go and not leave things for "later," because in this case, later often means never. You use the scissors, you put them right back. You bag up some carrots, you put away the big bag of carrots and the baggies. You play a game with the children, you all clean up. Sounds simple, right? Try it out; it isn't so simple. Your mind will already be on the next task at hand, as you silently promise to be right back in three minutes to clean

DON'T PUT IT DOWN

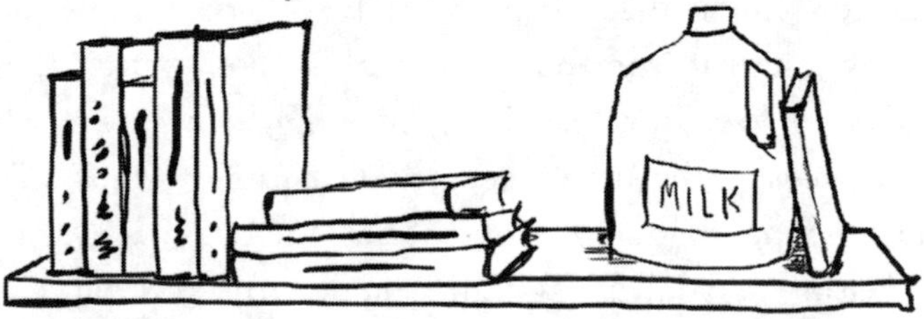

PUT IT AWAY

up the coffee beans that spilled on the counter as you were grinding your coffee. Before you know it, the laundry is on, the dinner is in the slow cooker, you called your great aunt for her birthday, and then you walk back into the kitchen and think, "Which lazy slob left coffee beans all over the place?" Oops. That was you. So take my Aunt Valerie's advice: *Don't put it down; put it away.* And while you're at it, wipe down the table after you finish eating.

Putting a few small, solid systems in place that are fixed to your routine can help you with the daily clean-as-you-go cleaning. You know the drill: Toothpaste cap back on the toothpaste, make your bed after you get out of it, put your shoes away as soon as you take them off. It comes easily to some and is a struggle for others. But the bottom line is that when you follow these sensible measures, your environment immediately looks so much better. I can hear you saying, "Well, how can I organize my sock drawer when the children have to be driven to school in three minutes?" Please, make a distinction between organizing the drawers in your home and clearing up your messy trail. You don't need to put checklists on the walls reminding you to put the lid back on the peanut butter and the phone back on the charging base. Rather, this involves a small paradigm shift in which your present self, who is talking on the phone, understands the feelings of your future self, who will be super frustrated when the phone dies in the middle of a conversation later that evening. So simply (or not so simply) remind yourself that your future self will be so much calmer in a clutter-free, organized environment.

KIND OF BORING, KIND OF PREDICTABLE CLEAN-AS-YOU-GO TIPS

- Clean up after yourself in the bathroom.
- Clean up after yourself in the bedroom.
- Clean up after yourself in the kitchen.
- Done eating? Rinse your dishes and give the floor a quick sweep.
- Your mom doesn't work here.
- You get the drift, right?

Daily Medium-Level Cleaning. Now that you've learned the benefits of cleaning up after yourself as you go, you can move on to daily medium-level cleaning. This might be something you outsource to a part-time or full-time cleaner, or you might share duties with your spouse or just take care of it yourself. Either way, most of our homes need a daily cleaning. Make a daily schedule for your home, and make sure there is someone to take care of it daily. It doesn't have to take a long time, but you will be amazed at the difference it makes if you can commit to doing it every day. Here's a sample checklist for daily medium-level cleaning:

Bedrooms
- Make beds.
- Clear clutter from the floor.

Bathroom
- Wipe down toilet and sinks.
- Clear clutter from the floor.

Kitchen/Dining Area
- Clear counters.
- Clean counters.
- Clear/wipe down breakfast table.
- Start the dishwasher.
- Sweep the floor.

Living Area
- Clear clutter off the floor and couches.

Miscellaneous
- Take out the garbage and recycling.
- Move the mail pile off piano and into your home office.

Weekly Deep Cleaning. In order for your home to look like a home and for you to feel somewhat relaxed as you walk into it, it needs to get deeply cleaned during the course of the week. Some people have a cleaner who will clean from top to bottom; others do it themselves. Someone, whether it is you or your delegated other, has to clean all surfaces that get touched, dropped on, and played on. Make sure you have good cleaning supplies on hand and a simple schedule too.

Monthly or Bimonthly Deep Cleaning. This is when the underside of the high chair gets scrubbed down and the patio get de-cluttered (again) and hosed down. It is when the stickiest shelves in the kitchen get cleaned and when the corners of your closet get hand-cleaned with a wipe, along with the air conditioner filters. You will need to create a more specific list for your home, and that list will liberate you.

Annual "Spring" Cleaning. Once a year, you should really clean the entire house from top to bottom. Traditionally, this is thought of as spring cleaning, but if you'd rather do it in August or February, go for it. Ship the kids out of the house, hire a cleaning service with your annual garage sale proceeds, or redeem some awesome Groupon for a cleaning service and get to work. Scrub and clean everything, and, of course, throw and give away as many of those clutter bugs as possible.

3. How Can You Remember the System?

Write everything down. Put it in your computer so you can revise it when needed, and print it out as often as possible for anyone who wants to (or is being paid to) help.

4. How Can You Keep the System Alive?

After a few months, reassess your systems to see if they are set up for success and if you can make them any simpler. Figure out what might be standing in the way of more efficient cleaning. Are you not vacuuming your upstairs often enough because you keep the vacuum downstairs and it hurts your back to schlep it up the stairs? Consider buying a second vacuum. If you don't have the funds for that right now, make a calendar note to check out Craigslist each Tuesday at 8:00 p.m. for five minutes until you land an incredible deal on a Dyson from someone who is moving to New Zealand.

TIP: A WINNING CLEANING SOLUTION: WHAT CAN MARINATE?

Whenever possible, let tough-to-clean items marinate. The pot you burned? Don't stand there scrubbing; let it soak overnight and then scrub. Your toilets? Splash in the cleaning solution before you leave the house and let it sit. Ditto the white shirt with the stain; let it marinate in pretreatment solution.

SORTING OUT THE LAUNDRY: A WEEKLY SYSTEM THAT WORKS

Laundry can be overwhelming for the best of us. The members of your family just keep putting on and taking off clothes every single day, don't they? Add another kid and another and another, and you risk disappearing behind the mounds of dirty socks. You need a laundry system with some predictability and routine. Then you won't have to think about it. And you won't be shocked by your daughter running into the kitchen to report that she has no clean underwear ten minutes before the bus arrives.

1. What Is Your Vision?

Basically, you want to make sure that all your laundry gets done on a regular basis and doesn't pile up into unmanageable mountains.

2. How Can You Achieve That Vision?

A laundry system should be simple enough that anyone can follow it. Put laundry hampers in every room, and require your kids (and your husband) to put their dirty clothes in them. Create a chart with the who, what, and when of laundry loads and stick one on the door of the laundry room and/or above the washing machine. This chart should account for when you change and wash sheets on all the beds, when you change and wash towels, and when the different types of clothing (darks, lights, uniforms, pants) or the different individuals' clothing gets washed.

Depending on the size of your family, your schedule may have everyone's clothes mixed all together, maybe sorted by color or fabric, or it may have different people assigned to different days. Do what works for you and what makes the most sense for your family.

A note on socks: It is a common enough problem that it has become a cliché: The dryer ate my sock. Well, your dryer is not actually eating the other sock; it is just getting lost somewhere between the foot and the clean clothes basket. Particularly if you have several kids close in age who wear similar socks or a husband who only ever wears the same black dress socks, you may want to institute a system of using mesh bags or sock locks to ensure that two socks come off the feet and two (matching) socks go back into the drawer. Here's how it works in my house (where seven children generate *a lot* of dirty socks):

> **Step #1.** Buy sock locks or sock bags and place them in an easily accessible place near your laundry bins.
>
> **Step #2.** Tell your children that socks need to be locked after they come off their feet in order to get washed (younger children may need help).
>
> **Step #3.** Wash and dry only the socks that are locked.
>
> **Step #4.** Place the socks back in drawers with or without the locks.
>
> **Step #5.** Repeat.

3. How Can You Remember the System?

Create a chart and stick it on the wall or above the washing machine.

4. How Can You Keep the System Alive?

While you will generally be able to stick to your system if it makes sense (and if it doesn't, tweak it), remember that there will be weeks when you have to deviate a bit from the plan. It may be because you are doing something fun one weekend and don't want to have to do laundry. In that case, maybe do an extra load on Thursday to give yourself the weekend off. Or if you have an unexpected accident or a particularly messy afternoon, do an extra load, but do not mix it in with other loads.

CASE STUDY
Lucy and the Laundry

LUCY was getting very overwhelmed with the laundry situation in her home. With three little girls, aged two, four, and seven, and no official laundry system in place, she was engulfed in despair when she saw the mounds of laundry piling up. This feeling of helplessness was exacerbated during the morning rush, when she could see the missing items from her children's outfits languishing in the heap of dirty laundry.

Lucy is a freelance editor, and she felt obliged to use the precious time when the girls were asleep to make headway in her work. Her husband was finishing up his medical residency, and there would be no cleaning help in the budget for the next eighteen months. She really needed a system.

1. What Is Your Vision?

When we met, it was clear that not having a smart system in place was making Lucy feel really bad about herself as a mother. She needed to take control of her laundry, so that she didn't have to waste time thinking about it or, worse, feeling guilty about it. So I began by asking Lucy to stop thinking so emotionally and put on her CEO thinking cap instead, the same cap that works really well for her when she is on assignment and under deadline.

2. How Can You Achieve That Vision?

We bought cute laundry hampers for each daughter and created a schedule that covered all the basics for the entire family:

Monday/Thursday	Bedding and towels and laundry of daughters A and B
Tuesday/Friday	Bedding and towels and laundry of daughter C
Wednesday/Sunday	Bedding and towels and laundry of Lucy and her husband

3. How Can You Remember the System?

Lucy printed out the schedule and put it on the door of her laundry room.

4. How Can You Keep the System Alive?

Glowing in the aftermath of her newly organized system, Lucy made a recurring note in her calendar to put in fifteen minutes every Thursday evening to tweak the system, if necessary, and keep it up and running.

I spent the first half of my life wondering who I was going to marry and the second half wondering what I was going to make for dinner.

— ERMA BOMBECK

MEAL PLANNING: NO MORE "MOM! WHAT'S FOR DINNER!?"

Meal planning has very little to do with actual cooking. It's choosing the meal and buying the supplies that take the bulk of the effort involved in getting meals on the table. Some women have bookshelves of cookbooks, plus a bulging folder of recipes that family and friends have sent them. Picking out a week's worth of menus can be tedious when you've got thousands of recipes to choose from. Add to the equation your own family's likes and dislikes, and the weekly reports on the pros and cons of various foods (have the experts agreed yet on whether eggs are good for you or bad for you?), and what's a good mother to do?

1. What Is Your Vision?

Here it is: You need a simple weekly meal plan so that you can buy the correct ingredients ahead of time and know exactly what is for dinner before you've even had your morning coffee.

2. How Can You Achieve That Vision?

The magic number is five. Planning ahead is the key to sanity. You need five weekday dinners.

Think Simple. Step away from the cookbooks and Aunt Sue's heirloom Swiss roll recipe. Those are fine when you have the time or are planning a dinner party. But for everyday dinners, you need to scale back. Think of five relatively straightforward suppers that you have prepared and your family has enjoyed. Consider a soup, a salad or green vegetable, a protein, and a carbohydrate. Write them down.

MEAL PLANNING

Now play with the results. Make sure there is some semblance of variety, and add all the spinach and alfalfa you want. Feel free to create a mixture of oven-ready and home-cooked suppers, such as fish sticks, rice, green beans, and minestrone soup. The goal isn't to restrict your creativity; it is to empower you by getting you ahead. If one day you are inspired to make a gourmet dish and you have the time and energy, go for it and ignore what you had planned to make. For some people, mentally designating one day a week as "gourmet night" works as well, although make sure you have some chicken nuggets in the freezer in case Cordon Bleu morphs into Cordon Burnt.

Tailor Meals to Different Family Members. Create meals where there is "spillover"—for example, where the soup and vegetables are the same but the carbohydrate and protein are different. Keep the fish sticks for the children, but grill some nice halibut for you and your husband. Make the children their pasta with butter, and boil yourselves some quinoa. And then serve everybody the same soup or vegetables. That way you are not totally reinventing the wheel. On a different note, children often need to be introduced to a new food several times. So maybe try to serve them the halibut, but dress it up with ketchup, cheese, or anything else that makes it feel less intimidating.

There are two kinds of people in this world:
those who love the slow cooker, and those who
don't know what the fuss is all about.

— KRISTIN VAN OGTROP

Make a Chart. Write or type the key ingredients next to the supper choice, and take the "key ingredients" column with you to the store. This will maximize the effectiveness of your food shopping time (see next section). Each week, look at your family's schedule and match the suppers to the day. If you are going to a dinner next Tuesday with your husband, you might skip the roast chicken your husband loves and instead make store-bought chicken fingers for your children.

Day	Supper	Key Ingredients
Monday	Lentil soup	Lentils, spinach, carrots
	Roast chicken and sweet potato	Chicken, sweet potato
	Fresh salad	Lettuce, cucumber, tomato, alfalfa sprouts, dressing
	Fruit	Watermelon

Pick a Time to Cook. Now make an entry in your calendar with a time when you will prepare the ingredients. Are you an early bird, a night owl, or something in between? Commit to a consistent time; you can always change it when you need to. Keep consulting your menu plan; some food will need to defrost, while other items will need to marinate. Some people cook and freeze in bulk, which is a fabulous time and energy saver. Cooking double portions and freezing the extra is simple yet effective.

Buy Early in the Week. Buy as many of your ingredients over the weekend or first thing in the week, and top up if you run out of fresh produce on Thursday or Friday. All that last-minute dashing to stores to buy fresh produce is wasting precious energy.

Repeat, Tweak, Repeat. After your first week, write some notes on the side, as you'll be using the first week's menus as a blueprint for week 3. For example, "Make vegetable soup with double the amount of carrots." Now create another five suppers for week 2. Follow the style of week 1, just altering things enough to prevent boredom. Roast chicken from week 1 can become barbecued chicken on week 2. Mushroom salmon on week 1 can become breaded flounder on week 2. Think simple.

Customize. Now you have a basic two-week menu plan. If you want to create a new menu plan for each week, that is your choice, but you now have the outline for a tried-and-true, pain-free menu plan. Consider cooking double portions on week 1 and freezing half so that you don't have to cook the same thing again for week 3. Customize your plan so that it works for you.

3. How Can You Remember the System?

Easy—you've already got the chart.

4. How Can You Keep the System Alive?

Keep making notes about things you might want to change, add, or delete. After a while, you will have it down. When your family gets bored, you can consider adapting your meal plan a bit to add some variety. As your younger children acquire more eclectic tastes and you think of more efficient ways to synthesize your meals, adjust your plan.

CASE STUDY
Dinner with Rochelle

ROCHELLE is a mom of two who enjoys cooking gourmet dinners. Yet, with her daughter home all day, her A.D.D., and an Italian vegetable market around the corner, she felt that there were so many choices for dinner that she got stymied. Invariably, she ended up making mac and cheese several nights a week, as her children would eat it without a fuss. She would often then make a second dinner for herself and her husband.

1. What Is Your Vision?

Rochelle needed a system so that she knew what to make each night, and could stop wasting time and energy and losing her love of cooking.

2. How Can You Achieve That Vision?

We created a weekly meal-plan chart with a different protein choice for each meal, a basic salad, and a different starch and vegetable. Soup was served during cold months and when Rochelle had become comfortable freezing parts of her meals ahead of time.

Day	Protein	Starch	Veg	Soup
Mon	Chicken	Sweet potatoes	Broccoli	Split pea
Tues	Fish	Rice	Asparagus	Minestrone
Wed	Beef Bolognese	Spaghetti	Cauliflower	Zucchini
Thurs	Mac and cheese	Mac and cheese	Corn on the cob	Lentil
Fri	Chicken	Potatoes	Green beans	Chicken

The chart gave more structure to Rochelle's meal planning. We also agreed on a new "when," whereby the dinner had to be prepped by 10:00 a.m., which enabled her to walk with her daughter to the nearby vegetable market either the afternoon before or the morning of planning. The cooking could be done either in the morning or the afternoon, as that took no energy as long as she was home.

3. How Can You Remember the System?
Rochelle printed out the chart and stuck it on her fridge.

4. How Can You Keep the System Alive?
I suggested to Rochelle that she could tweak the menu every Sunday, but I advised her to stick to the same protein choices. On Sundays that were too busy for her to make changes to the meal plan, Rochelle just stuck to the original menu.

GROCERY SHOPPING: SANITY CHECK IN AISLE 7

The odds of going to the store for a loaf of bread and coming out with only a loaf of bread are three billion to one.

— ERMA BOMBECK

The freedom that meal planning gives you also enables you to have freedom with your shopping. We spend way too much time either making shopping lists that omit the key items or leaving the list at home and trying to shop from our heads. That is fine if you live in

Tuscany and swing by the local market as you bike into town each day. However, for most of us, our inefficient shopping ways are taking up precious nuggets of time that could be spent more wisely. Whip a super-efficient system into place, and then catch up with friends for coffee or take that tai chi class instead. And you'll still have the energy to do the voices for your kid's bedtime story.

1. What Is Your Vision?

Basically, you want to streamline your shopping so it gets done in as little time as possible, with as little stress as possible, and without forgetting to buy peanut butter.

2. How Can You Achieve That Vision?

To make your shopping quicker and more effective, you can create inventory lists for the items you buy in each of the shops you patronize. For example, if you divide your shopping among the Stop & Shop, Whole Foods, and Trader Joe's (because they each have something different that you can't live without), you should know exactly what you buy where and which store has the better deal on any items available in more than one place. Design your lists so that they mirror the layout of the store. Then you can leave the list on the fridge (or on your iPad) and check off a particular item when you run out of something. The night before you go shopping, you can also walk around your kitchen checking off the items you need.

Check your local store's websites; some have their items listed by aisle, and others even provide a checklist. If not, consider making your own, such as the one on the following page. If you can't take the time to create the document in one shot, then consider creating it an aisle a week until the list is done.

Aisle #	Item	Amount
Aisle 1 : Produce	Cherry tomatoes	1
Aisle 1: Produce	European cucumber	2
Aisle 1: Produce	Pink Lady apples, 5lb bag	1
Aisle 2 : Cereals	Cheerios	1
Aisle 2 : Cereals	Oatmeal	2
Aisle 3 : Snacks	Granola bar, 6-pack assorted	1
Aisle 3 : Snacks	Organic applesauce, 6-pack	1

Another thing that will vastly improve the effectiveness of your grocery shopping is syncing it with your meal plan (you know, that awesome plan you created just a few pages ago). Once you have begun to organize your meals, you can also organize your shopping with a similar system. Your meal plan should have the grocery items needed right there ready for you to check off.

Even better, avoid the store altogether when you can and use a web-based grocery delivery service. If there is one available to you that is relatively simple to use, I highly recommend it. The extra few dollars you spend on delivery will probably be no more than the cost of the random items you would have picked up spontaneously had you gone to the store yourself. Book a standard delivery time, have your basic weekly list on record to be ordered automatically, and add the necessary extra items via a phone call.

You can also get a lot of items delivered by ordering from the Internet. Amazon's "subscribe and save" feature gives you discounted prices and free shipping if you sign up for automated delivery. From cat litter to spelt flour, it is worth checking out the nonperishable items you can order there to make your shopping easier.

A final suggestion for those who absolutely loathe the grocery store, or could really use that precious time for something else, is to outsource grocery shopping altogether. Consider paying someone to do your shopping for you. Hand or email them your checklist and ask them to hide a chocolate bar in your glove compartment. If you find this hard to do on a weekly basis, then consider hiring someone when you are having a big event coming up or if a child is sick.

3. How Can You Remember the System?

Make a note on your paper or digital calendar for a couple of days before the shopping day to remind you to check if there are any new items you need to add to the standard weekly list. And keep your list in a really accessible place (the front of the fridge works well), so that you can't help but write down that item before you forget it.

4. How Can You Keep the System Alive?

Often your week will be too crazy you to take the precious time to do inventory, so even if you have carved out time for the shopping or outsourced it to someone wonderful, the bottom line is that you don't have the right stuff on your list! If you find that this keeps happening to you, consider creating a new system that needs less attention (gosh, those lists can be so needy). How about creating a slim basic list of what you need every week? You could combine that with software such as Basecamp that lets you email in the items you are running out of (that's the equivalent of the checklist on the front of the fridge for people on the go).

Some weeks will be more organized than others, but that's the dance we dance. When you goof, either learn a lesson for next time or order pizza (or both).

GETTING OUT THE DOOR WITH KIDS: IF YOU ARE NOT EARLY, YOU ARE LATE

Going anywhere with children resembles a small military procedure. Wipes? Check. Snacks? Check. Bathroom stops? Check.

It can get somewhat anxiety-provoking when you know your cousin and her new fiancé are waiting for you at a restaurant and you are on all fours looking under the couch for the pink glow-in-the-dark pacifier that your daughter is crying for. While I can't wave my magic wand and make everything better from now onward, I can give you three tips that have saved my sanity.

1. Get as much ready twenty-four hours ahead of time as possible.

2. Differentiate between the time you are going to start loading the children into the car and the time you aim to pull away. The former is your "load time."

3. Plan your load time for ten minutes earlier than you need to actually pull out of the driveway. That way, if you have to turn back for the aforementioned pacifier, you can smile and roll your eyes as opposed to busting a coronary artery over it.

TAMING THE MORNING MADNESS

Want a surefire recipe for a calm and relaxing morning? Send the children out of the house to sleep over at their grandparents' or friends' houses and pull the covers back over your head. However, if the children are actually spending the night in your home, forget any notion of tranquil mornings. What you can do, however, is institute a slew of systems to make mornings manageable, so that you are using your time and energy only for the essentials.

TAMING THE MORNING MADNESS

If you are choosing to make three different breakfasts, prepare two lunch boxes full of snacks and lunches, wait the ten minutes for clean underwear to come out of the dryer, fix the quirky printer so it prints out the essay your son needs to hand in today, and get gas—all before you drop the kids at school—don't come crying to me if your mornings provide you with three weeks' worth of stress and anxiety.

1. What Is Your Vision?

Does your vision involve sunlight hitting the breakfast table, where your smiling and well-scrubbed children are politely eating their hot cooked breakfasts and not fighting at all? Well, yeah, mine does too. Now let's get realistic. What you want is relative calm in the mornings, so that everyone can get up, get dressed, get fed, and head off to school or work with everything they need and without you (or someone else in your family) losing your mind or losing your cool.

2. How Can You Achieve That Vision?

Remember this: *The morning starts the night before, and the night before starts the weekend before.* Take a look at your mornings and see what can be done ahead of time. Clothing, snacks, lunches, and all homework should be taken care of the night or weekend before. Create snack closets, lunch systems, and closet organizers that lend themselves to be set up in bulk.

Breakfast. Breakfast can be a real challenge for the best of us. The children often aren't particularly hungry, and if they do grace you with the honor of liking boiled eggs one day, there is no guarantee they will eat them any other day that week. So when the planets align and your son eats a whole bowl full of whole-grain oatmeal, don't try to figure out whether it is worth your while to order oatmeal by the ton. Just smile sweetly and make a mental note that oatmeal can be revisited next week.

To improve breakfast in your home, sit down with the children and create a weekly breakfast schedule. Take notes, as this lets them know you are taking this seriously. Keep it healthy and keep it simple. You can come up with some bribery, such as chocolate chip pancakes on Sunday morning if they eat their breakfast during the week, or even a simple reward system. Encourage your children to think outside the box; some kids might be very happy to eat dinner leftovers for breakfast! An essential component is making sure you have the adequate supplies and also that you do as much as possible the night before.

A WEEK OF SIMPLE BREAKFASTS

Monday: Instant oatmeal (with chopped fruit and/or nuts)

Tuesday: Banana and peanut butter toast

Wednesday: Boiled eggs and rice cakes

Thursday: Cereal and milk

Friday: Applesauce muffin

Snacks and Lunches. Preparing snacks and lunches to send to school with your kids is another system you can create ahead of time with the children. They will complain and tell you that *e-v-e-r-y-o-n-e* brings cooler snacks or lunches than them. Nod sympathetically and throw in some extra baby carrots to up the vitamin A quotient of your child's candy-consuming classmates.

For lunches, you can make a weekly schedule, just as you do for breakfast and dinner. Sit down with your kids and talk about what they want in their lunch boxes. Make categories of basic lunch components, such as a main course (a sandwich, cheese and crackers, leftover pasta), a fruit and/or veggies (grapes, an apple, baby carrots, celery sticks), and snacks (pretzels, chips, whatever your kids like), and come up with combinations for each day. If you make two or three weeks' worth of lunch schedules, you can rotate them and the kids will not get bored. Load up on supplies ahead of time, and set aside time each night to prepare snacks and lunches. In our home, an alarm rings at 6:30 p.m. to give the children ten minutes in the kitchen to prepare their snacks and lunches and clean up after themselves.

3. How Can You Remember the System?

Work out your plan, write it up on a chart, and stick it up on the fridge for future reference.

4. How Can You Keep the System Alive?

If you are finding the same uneaten thing in your child's lunch box every day after school, the best system in the world won't make him eat it. After a few weeks, tweak the system to make sure the food you are sending to school is actually being eaten. And commit to making those lunches every evening, even if you are tired and think it could just wait until morning. After a while, it will become second nature.

RESTORING SANITY TO
YOUR EVENINGS

Evenings would be so much simpler if they could take place in the morning! The children are tired after a long day in school, and they are cranky because they don't like dinner, are overtired, or lost their ball, or because no one likes them (if not all of the above). You've had a long day, which began at 4:00 a.m. when your child woke you because of nightmares, and by the time you soothed him back to sleep, you were wide awake. You began your day way too early, and your patience quota is that of a four-year-old. So what's the magic answer?

While I don't claim to have perfected this one yet, I think I know how you feel on those nights where nothing is falling into place. Imagine your sanity as the last small amount of charge remaining on your cell phone. You were out all day running errands, unable to plug in your phone, and now you see that you have maybe ten minutes of talk time left. You need your kids, husband, BFF in crisis, or boss to be able to reach you, so you have to be super vigilant about guarding that last small bit of phone life. No random calls, and for sure no battery-draining photos of funny license plates to post on your Facebook wall.

Same too with your evenings. There will be some evenings when your patience quota is fully charged and you are able to juggle the sautéing chicken, the science project, and the "everyone hates me" monologue. And there will be other evenings when you feel totally drained and the ever-so-empathetic conversation you are having with your four-year-old over her broken toy is taking all the patience you never thought you had.

Bedtimes are challenging for parents and children; we are exhausted, and so are the children. They get cranky, we get cranky. We want to help them finish their schoolwork and drift happily off to sleep; they want *all* of our focus and patience. This section is a

RESTORING

SANITY

TO YOUR
EVENING

good fit for newborns through tweens, although certain tips will be relevant for dealing with your child at any age.

⁓❉⁓

When you teach your child, you are actually

teaching your grandchild.

—THE TALMUD

1. What Is Your Vision?

Just as you wouldn't venture through the mosquito-infested, alligator-filled Everglades without a guide or a GPS, so too you need a system and a schedule for the evenings to allow you to make it to a happy morning with your sanity intact. Aside from saving your soul, having an evening schedule will also allow you to have easier, more fulfilling time with your children on a regular basis.

2. How Can You Achieve That Vision?

A tired mom is not a surprise. Think of how early our days begin and the myriad of responsibilities that we attend to until bedtime. It is enough to make children clear up after themselves, put their school bags by the front door, brush their teeth, and quietly pop off to sleep—we wish!

Here is the brutal truth that I am sure will ruffle some feathers: Quite honestly, it really isn't their problem that we are tired. We are the parents and they are the children, and it is our responsibility to parent them. What I highly recommend is that you set a schedule that circumnavigates their total meltdown and gets them to bed early enough in the evening that you still have time for you. Review those bedtimes and make them earlier if you possibly can, and yes, there is no crime in putting your kids down exactly at the moment the clock chimes their bedtime. You are saving them from Crazy Mom (that is you, by the way, when you are tired and cranky). So work on doing things earlier, give yourself a mid-afternoon break, if possible, and chug down some protein (or caffeine?) to give you that extra boost and remind yourself that you are the parent.

The more systems you have in place, the more of a safety net you will have to fall back on. The following is a list of the key goals most families strive for. Aim for all of the following as the *destination*. If you are currently unable to achieve any of these, then pick one of them; once you have it taken care of it, add another.

1. Have the house presentable.
2. Have your dinner prepared ahead of time.
3. Have clear schedules (with some flexibility) for the evenings.
4. Have set bedtimes, with rewards for being in bed on time.
5. Have systems in place for doing homework, organizing backpacks, and preparing the next day's snacks and lunches that save you from being the appointed sergeant major.

Additionally, embrace your inner flight attendant. Think about how those folks prepare the cabin for an evening flight. They lower the lights, hand out bedding, and speak in hushed tones. Do the same in your home; no child is going to drift off to sleep when surrounded by bright lights, loud conversations, and loud music. Dim the lights, get the phone users in the home to step outside for loud calls, and start to speak in hushed tones. Some mothers use lavender oil in baths or dotted on pillows to facilitate their little ones falling off to sleep. Yes, your friends without children will consider you officially insane, but remember the goal: The children need the sleep, and the children need to go to sleep feeling loved and nurtured.

According to sleep expert Dr. Marc Weissbluth, most children are not getting enough sleep, which is a lose-lose for parents and children alike. Putting our children to sleep later than their bodies can handle also results in a much harder bedtime for us. Talk about a frustrating situation to be in. The trick is to work out your child's ideal bedtime and work backward.

Take a look at the time your child has to be up the next morning and plan your evening by working backward. Some of you may already have a stellar evening routine in place; others may not have established one yet. I highly recommend creating one. It truly helps children go to sleep soundly, as they feel comforted and relaxed by the predictability of their evening routine.

Here is an example of an evening schedule for a five-year-old, who should be pretty much sleeping by 7:00 p.m. Adapt this to accurately reflect your lifestyle and give it a whirl. Create your own time line, working backward, then use that framework to establish a new and improved evening routine. The beauty is in going back to the basics of a predictable routine, with the win-win result that the child gets put to sleep before he gets overtired and unreasonable and before Mom and Dad start getting cranky and miserable also.

So working backward toward that sweet goal . . .

Child in bed falling asleep	7:00 p.m.
Read book, sing bedtime song, say good night to the moon, say bedtime prayer	6:40 p.m.
Tidy up room and set out clothes for the next day	6:30 p.m.
Bath time and teeth-brushing time	6:10 p.m.
Finish dinner and clear off plates	6:00 p.m.
Dinner	5:40 p.m.

Make sure to set the atmosphere by dimming lights, removing loud toys, playing soft music, and limiting loud phone calls.

Once you have more than one child, their schedules should have some overlap and some time for individual attention, and each child should have an actual bedtime that changes as he or she gets older.

3. How Can I Remember the System?

Post those bedtimes and the evening routine in a highly visible location, and cling to it as if your sanity depends on it, because, well, it does.

4. How Can I Keep the System Alive?

After a few weeks of bedtime consistency, it should become much easier, both at night and the following morning.

Of course, the universe—along with family functions, holidays, teething/sick children, and tween issues—will challenge your resolve to stick to your bedtime routine. Try to the best of your ability to stick to the schedule, but of course we don't want your child to miss your brother's wedding either. Use your skill as your family's CEO to assess when to deviate from your system; just know that the following day you will need extra resolve to get the system back on track. Or perhaps, if you are super lucky, your child will be exhausted enough to fall asleep before he gets the energy to give you a run for your money.

On the nights when you can't stick to the schedule, tweak other variables to make bedtime go as smoothly as possible. Order in dinner, forget bath time, and put your children's clothes in their hampers for them. As I have said before, *a good CEO does not live or die by sticking to her systems. It is knowing when letting them slide will benefit the greater good that makes you smart.* Remember that the goal is to get the children to sleep feeling loved and nurtured.

MOM'S RELAXATION TIME

Relaxation isn't just pleasant.
It promotes abstract thinking.

—MICHEL TUAN PHAM

Yes, you read that heading right. You need to systemize *your* evenings as well. You shouldn't be passing out on the couch with the field trip permission form in your hand; you should be doing the same thing as your children: working out what time you want to be asleep and then working the timing backward to ensure that you get in some relaxation time and "me time" beforehand.

1. What Is Your Vision?

There are always going to be crazy nights when you have to be at three different events in one evening, but there are also going to be evenings when you end up scratching your head at midnight and wondering where all the time went. Evenings are just like the children's toys: they need to be corralled or else they will be all over the place. You need to make sure that once you've gotten the children in bed, you will have some time to unwind and finish your day in peace before you go to sleep.

2. How Can You Achieve That Vision?

Just as the setting of the sun behind the horizon line is a gradual process, so too is the sunset in our minds. At a certain point, there has to be a crossover when one day is over and the evening begins. Give yourself a rough timetable for the evenings: You are busy with the children and your home until a certain point; then the phone gets turned off and recharged, and you start to turn off from the activities of today and tomorrow and recharge.

Come up with a time that you would love to be relaxing and winding down and work backward. Let's say you aim to be in the bath or in your bed with a book by 9:30 p.m. Or maybe you and your husband want to catch up on the latest episode of *Survivor* at that time. Set your alarm on your phone for 9:00 p.m. That's when you turn off your phone and get serious about closing up shop. If you haven't done so already as part of your awesome evening system, make the lunches, sign the notes, and get the children's clothes ready. If your children are older and still awake then, let them know that there are no more homework questions or permission slips signed after 9:00, and take care of anything that is going to bother you in the bath or your bed or in front of the TV. If you are consistent about going off duty at a certain time each night, your children will learn to understand. Allow them to text you or stick a note under your door. Of course, there will be times when they need to disturb you for something important, and that's OK. But as a general rule, let them learn the importance of Mom time.

3. How Can You Remember the System?

Keep that alarm set on your phone, and make sure to integrate your personal bedtime routine with the family's general evening schedule and the children's bedtime system, so that your evenings flow smoothly right up until the moment your head hits the pillow.

4. How Can You Keep the System Alive?

It is going to be a struggle to remove yourself each evening, as there will always be more things to be done. However, once you've been consistent about relaxing for a week, you will notice a difference in the quality of your sleep and a higher level of concentration the following day. That's when you will realize that the time you take to relax pays you back. By thinking of all of your brain cells rejuvenating, you will feel more inclined to leave the day behind and jump into a warm bath. Feel free to invest in some yummy bath goodies to help coax you away from checking email and into the warm, soapy suds.

CASE STUDY
Bassy's Bedtime

BASSY is an awesome mom of four young children, two of whom are home with her all day. Needless to say, her days were hectic. After the children were all asleep, she used the evening time to get ahead on the laundry, light cleaning, and prepping clothes and lunches for the following day. Once she had done that for a couple of hours, she would have every good intention of relaxing and unwinding, but she would invariably fall asleep on the couch or literally drop onto her bed.

1. What Is Your Vision?
After running around all day, Bassy needed time in the evening to relax, unwind, and pamper herself.

2. How Can You Achieve That Vision?
A mother's work is never done, and we don't have the luxury of walking out of our "offices" and leaving work behind until tomorrow. But by leveraging her time during the day more

effectively, Bassy would be able to feel her work was done and could allow herself to relax in the evenings. After driving the older two children to school, Bassy still had her two little ones at home with her. I recommended that she give the little guys breakfast, set out a few toys, and leverage their early-morning mellowness to prep dinner and put in a load of laundry. By creating systems for dinner and laundry, Bassy would be able to keep those systems going without too much effort. For example, if her system told her that on Monday she would be washing her oldest child's clothes and linens and putting a chicken dish into the slow cooker, she could get it done with little thought. I also advised her to leverage naptime. Bassy put both babies down to sleep at the same time, so I advised her to use half of the naptime to do light cleaning and set out clothes for the next day and the other half to give herself a catnap or relax with a book.

3. How Can You Remember the System?

With so many little people depending on her, Bassy would really benefit from as many systems as possible, which would lead to more effective house management, which in turn would help her finish her work day earlier and be able to get down to relaxing earlier. So I encouraged her to implement as many systems as possible, write them down, and post them in visible spots.

4. How Can You Keep the System Alive?

Bassy has to be vigilant throughout the day so that her work is done by the time her oldest child goes to sleep, to ensure her that precious pocket of relaxation. But after a while, she will be benefiting from the extra relaxation time so much that she will be very invested in protecting it.

FAMILY RULES AS PUBLIC POLICY

Now that you have started to implement some wholesome systems in your world and are reaping the benefits of a more stable environment, how about doing what any diligent CEO would do and implementing the systems as public policy? Except, instead of handing your employees a fat rule book that will gather dust under their desks, simply condense them into a few simple rules and put them up on the wall. That gives you the freedom to refer to them whenever you need to and will get you off the hook when you have to make a controversial ruling. "Honey, of course you want to sleep with your sister's new doll under your pillow, but our family rules say you can't." And here's an even better perk: You get to take down the sign and change public policy whenever you see fit. Love it!

One way to help ensure that the rules are respected by all members of your family is to introduce them at a family meeting. Go over them together and establish them together. (Of course, you've already decided what the rules will be, but if you give your children the illusion of being a part of creating the rules, they are more likely to follow them!)

One family I know came up with these eight "golden rules" for their home. I think they say it all:

OUR FAMILY RULES[*]

① IF YOU VALUE IT, TAKE CARE OF IT.

② IF YOU USE IT, PUT IT BACK.

③ IF IT'S NOT BROKEN, DON'T FIX IT.

④ IF YOU WANT RESPECT, RESPECT OTHERS.

⑤ IF YOU MAKE A MESS, CLEAN IT UP.

⑥ IF IT BELONGS TO SOMEONE ELSE,
      GET PERMISSION TO USE IT.

⑦ IF IT'S NONE OF YOUR BUSINESS,
      DON'T ASK QUESTIONS.

⑧ IF IT WILL BRIGHTEN SOMEONE'S DAY,
      SAY IT.

* MANY THANKS TO THE LABER FAMILY.

SYSTEMIZE DATE NIGHT WITH DAD

Have you ever had a few weeks pass and realize that you haven't gone out with your husband or even had an actual conversation that didn't involve the children? Consider systemizing your date night into a weekly or bimonthly event; put it in the family calendar and book the babysitter well in advance. It may lack the spontaneity of your dating era, but that beats not having fun with your spouse for months on end.

TRAVELING: WHO LET THOSE CHILDREN ON THE PLANE?

If you look like your passport photo,
you're too ill to travel.

—WILL KOMM

It is a *major* headache to travel with little children. I am surprised that my parents ever took me anywhere. Just the mention of the word *travel* can reduce a grown woman to a sniveling heap in a fetal position, crying "Save me!" into her pillow. I even have friends who prefer not to go on vacation at all, just to save themselves the trauma of packing. Throw a couple of children into the mix, along with having to be the in-flight entertainment for a two-year-old for eight hours, a stroller that won't collapse, and two car seats to schlep through the airport and it is enough to give a parent nightmares for a month before the trip.

TRAVELING

The actual traveling is most likely the most painful element of travel. Think of it as if it were labor all over again, and then you won't be surprised by the amount of self-control it is going to take not to scream out loud every eight minutes with a toddler and an infant wiggling all over the place on the plane.

1. What Is Your Vision?

While traveling with the little ones isn't all fun and games, there is something to be said for going away with the family, even if you don't actually sleep for the entire week. The photos and the memories of you all at Disney World will stay on your wall and in your children's minds forever. It is a question of forward planning combined with a fresh attitude and a few tricks up your sleeve.

2. How Can You Achieve That Vision?

From the moment you leave your home until you arrive at your destination, you are the official party entertainment. So just accept that you are not going to get much reading done on the plane. Once you have had a paradigm shift, think about what you can do to make things simpler and divide up the duties with your husband. Feel free to take a book along; just don't assume you will get to read more than a page an hour.

Get Ahead. You and I both know that 90 percent of packing can be done three weeks early. I know it feels so unnecessary to do that, but do it anyway. Even if it means buying extra sets of underwear or socks, *do it*. Pack each family member's items into their own suitcase, or use big transparent zipper bags and have a couple of those bags in each suitcase. If you want to put entire outfits together for your children and wrap them individually with an elastic band, that also works.

Write It Down. The main thing is to shift your packing lists out of your mind and onto paper or your iPad screen. Challenge yourself to customize packing lists for each family member, attach the lists to clipboards, and start checking off the items you have already packed. By devoting as little as ten minutes a day to this, you can get loads packed and can reduce last-minute stress tremendously. Be really strict about including on the list any extra items that will need to be packed. These lists will not only save your sanity now but should be turned into living documents that are updated regularly and used again the next time you travel. You will be amazed at how better list making translates into better sleep.

Pack Less. By the way, while you're at it, pack 50 percent less stuff. Remember the last time you traveled and used only six of the twelve outfits you packed? Take items you love, and have your outfits coordinate somewhat into a capsule wardrobe so you can switch items around if need be. If you have too much stuff, you will pay overweight charges to the airline, and your hotel room will feel really claustrophobic.

One of my bucket list items is to go on vacation without packing and just stop off at a Target-type store while on vacation and buy everything I need. Then I will bring home the items I fell in love with in my carry-on and give the rest away to deserving people before leaving town. I know this is a bit extreme, but the main lesson to learn is that unless you are taking your children to a desert island, there are going to be shops there. There is something incredibly redeeming about not having to pack and reducing your carbon footprint at the same time.

Pack Smarter. Send your husband's shirts to the cleaner to get boxed up, and fold the rest of your clothing in a smart manner to reduce creasing. By keeping each family member's items together and packing ahead of time, you have the added luxury of not having to play "treasure hunt" for your clothing each morning of your vacation.

Vital Documents. You don't want to find out the night before a trip that any family member's passport expired last June. Right after you book your tickets, check out where all the passports are and when they expire. Trust me, the last-minute rush for passports can be harrowing. Been there, done that—and *not* doing it again.

One of the best things about traveling

is coming home.

—JULIET LANDAU-POPE

Leverage Parkinson's Law and Come Home to a Happier Home. One of the super-duper things about leveraging Parkinson's Law (a task expands to fill the time allotted) is that by packing ahead and not having a frazzled forty-eight hours prior to traveling, you can do something wonderful and unique: You can think over what your home needs while you are gone. Maybe you can set up a seep hose for the new flowers you planted, or go through the pile of papers on your desk so that you will come home to a clean desk and a feeling of empowerment. Maybe you can cook some dinners and freeze them to allow the freedom of a vacation to linger a little longer. You get the idea: By prepping for your return, you can extend the vacation bliss for just a little longer.

Pre-Travel, No-Anxiety Diet. The funny part about travel anxiety is that there really is nothing to be anxious about. Will your children act like perfect angels on the flight? Unlikely. Will you forget something? Highly likely. When you are aware of these two facts, you don't have to be anxious over the possibility of them happening, because you know they will. So just accept this reality—and breathe.

Entertainment Supplies. Take along light and compact supplies so you can pull tricks out of your hat when they're needed. If your children are older than three, you can make them their own bags with coloring books, stickers, etc. Snacks are a good form of entertainment, especially ones with a low sugar count. You should also travel with a package of small, multicolored stickers and Band-Aids to keep on hand for the landing and takeoff times, when the children have to be bribed to stay still. And if you wrap something, even if it is a tiny sheet of stickers or a pack of gum, it will seem immensely more exciting and special to your child.

3. How Can You Remember the System?

Travel is an area where getting ahead and making lists yield deep dividends. Also consider that something that takes a few moments now can save hours of aggravation later on.

4. How Can You Keep the System Alive?

The main thing to remember is to pack with your family in mind. Considering your family's individual needs can greatly reduce vacation stress. If your daughter always falls asleep with a white-noise maker, take one along, together with sufficient batteries. This is not the time for magically thinking, "Oh, the ocean breeze will knock her out." Ditto for her blankie, pacifier, and bottle. Keep it real, and you will reap serious benefits. Also, know your children and become a quick believer in the power of bribery. If you can get a tired toddler to walk for twenty minutes to the baggage-claim area, that might well be worth a small pack of Twizzlers.

This too shall pass.

—KING SOLOMON

PART III

NOW

WHAT?

Gold medals aren't really made of gold.
They're made of sweat, determination, and
a hard-to-find alloy called guts.

—DAN GABLE

NOW that you've set your priorities, cleared out the clutter, and implemented your fabulous new systemized life, how can you sustain it? In other words, you've got the plane in the air. Great—now keep it there.

Like any good diet or lifestyle change, the next part of your journey is maintenance. This is the tricky part, as it may seem tedious compared to all that liberation you felt while implementing your systems.

Just like a marathon runner, you are going to have to keep on running, even when it gets tough, boring, and sometimes painful, if you want the cheers and the runner's high when you pass that glorious finish line. Stay on track with your systems, and before you know it, they will become second nature. Then running through the seemingly "boring" parts won't be quite so tedious—especially when you understand the rewards waiting for you at the end.

When you are on the road to success,
it isn't time to take a nap.

—ANONYMOUS

The following three tips can help give you the skills and the encouragement you need to keep your eyes on the prize—namely, an organized life with less stress and more free time to focus on what you love and what matters most to you.

PRACTICE MAKES "GOOD ENOUGH"

PRACTICE MAKES "GOOD ENOUGH"

REMEMBER how we learned earlier in the book that you want your parachute to be packed perfectly, but the majority of other things can be done "well enough." Changing the patterns of a lifetime takes great courage. Consider becoming what Tal Ben-Shahar refers to as an "optimalist": Commit to being part of the elite group of recovering perfectionists who now lead rich and fulfilling lives by accepting the reality that very few things can really be done perfectly. These people accept failure as normal and natural; therefore they experience less anxiety and fewer disappointments in their everyday lives.

Living a more organized life is not about never failing; it's about having the strength to dust yourself off and carry on. I guarantee that you will have crazy days when even your best intentions lead to the exact results you were hoping to avoid. Frankly, if you're not occasionally making mistakes, then you're not trying hard enough. Sometimes the dinner you got up super early to make in the slow cooker will be sitting there as raw as can be when you get home, because you forgot to plug in the cooker. Learn the lesson for the future, forgive yourself for not being superhuman, have a good laugh, and give the children cereal for dinner.

So keep at it, even if it doesn't seem perfect and even if it is boring. After a while, you will wonder how—and why—you ever lived without your systems.

REFLECT, LOOK
AT RESULTS & TWEAK
WHEN NECESSARY

However beautiful the strategy, you should occasionally look at the results.

—WINSTON CHURCHILL

A successful CEO doesn't live or die by adhering to existing systems. If a staff picnic has been scheduled a year in advance and a tropical storm hits on the day of the picnic, the event will either be postponed or be held in a different venue. As the CEO of your home, you are in charge of a million systems that constantly need tweaking—meals, uniforms, laundry, toy storage—so be prepared and start thinking ahead now to incorporate some predetermined tweaks into your life. The thing about parenting is that nothing ever stays the same. You work out the dinner plan and someone develops an allergy. You work out the perfect car-pool system and your daughter decides she'd rather do gymnastics than swimming. Understand that such shifts are par for the course.

And every once in a while, take a good look at your systems to see if they are succeeding. Remember that a system is a living, breathing thing. Fancy charts and schedules might look nice tacked onto the door, but if they aren't producing your intended vision, something needs to be fixed. Try to figure out what is stopping your

TWEAK

WHEN

NECESSARY

system from working. Think outside the box for solutions or ask yourself the question taught to me by my colleague Roberta Shapiro: "Things worked out really well. What did you do that you should keep on doing?" Once you've figured out what the problem is, alter the system and get yourself back on track. And then keep on plugging away and keep on tweaking systems. On the other hand, if a system ain't broke, don't fix it.

SOME SYSTEMS SHOULD STAY IN PLACE, NO MATTER WHAT

Crises are inevitable, but totally falling apart and letting the house go to pot is optional. There are going to be days when you feel your family is conspiring to drive you insane. Of course, your deep cleaning of the kitchen cabinets doesn't have to be done if your son has been vomiting for a week, but choosing to not keep up with *any* of your systems is guaranteed to make you even crazier. Having no fresh laundry or fresh food to eat isn't going to make things calmer.

Decide what very basic systems your family needs pretty much every day and commit to sticking to them to the best of your ability. That may mean keeping a couple of frozen dinners in the freezer and knowing that throwing the occasional extra load of clothes into the washing machine will pay off the next morning.

There is beauty in the basics, and with these basics in place you will have an overall skeleton system in place that will preserve your sanity.

COZY UP
TO YOUR FUTURE SELF

The past is for your present good.

—RABBI DR. LAIBI WOLF

NOW that you are out of crisis mode and feeling less frazzled and more focused, concentrate on developing a healthy relationship with your future self. This concept is the time management equivalent of the adage "A latte spurned is a fortune earned." Recognize that everything you do today, every system you stick to, every commitment you keep will have a positive impact on your future self—and think about how much you will then appreciate the efforts of your present self.

If you have a trip planned with your toddlers, your future self (stuck on the plane with them) will very much appreciate the extra stickers and coloring books you brought along in their carry-on bags. Same too for the dress you are able to fit into for your son's bar mitzvah because you faithfully attended your weekly Pilates class. And imagine how much your exhausted future self will appreciate the fact that you planned Thursday night's dinner and bought all the necessary ingredients the previous weekend.

Conversely, if you choose not to plan dinners, not to use your laundry system, or not to put things back where they belong, just make sure that your present and future selves agree that it is worth the consequences. Feel free to rebel once in a while; just check in with your future self more often than not to make sure it will be worth it.

There are many, many people who believe themselves to be much less capable than they are in reality.

—RABBI DR. ABRAHAM TWERSKI

YOU ARE
NOT ALONE!

YOU did it! You made it to the end of the book. And I hope that, along the way, you did some serious thinking about the way you are managing your life and your home and your family. Maybe you have already implemented some fantastic systems that are making things run more smoothly in your home. Maybe you have some great new ideas and plans for systems that you will begin to implement in the coming weeks.

I am very proud of you.

And I am not leaving you on your own. If you liked the advice in this book and want more details and additional ideas, please check out my website (www.sobeorganized.com), where you can find lots more useful information. If you are looking for occasional tips and encouragement, follow me on Twitter (@sobeorganized) or Facebook (SoBe Organized). And if you are looking for kindred souls, great ideas that worked for other families, or just a place to vent about how your kids simply won't (fill in the blank), then join the chorus of other moms on my Frazzled to Focused Facebook page. Feel free to post questions, and I will use your current concerns as a focus on my online forums and might even surprise you with a direct response.

YOU ARE NOT ALONE

USEFUL RESOURCES

Books

Getting Things Done by David Allen

Lighten Up by Peter Walsh

Living the 80/20 Way by Richard Koch

Man's Search for Meaning by Viktor E. Frankl

No Regrets Parenting by Harley A. Rotbart

Organizing from the Inside Out by Julie Morgenstern

The Pursuit of Perfect by Tal Ben-Shahar

Rework by Jason Fried and David Heinemeier Hansson

The E-Myth Revisited by Michael E. Gerber

The One-Minute Organizer by Donna Smallin

The Paradox of Choice by Barry Schwartz

Throw Out Fifty Things by Gail Blanke

Websites

www.apartmenttherapy.com
A great website to browse if you are looking for clever and original ways to use and decorate your home.

www.flylady.net
A fun way to get email reminders and inspiration to help eliminate chaos from your life.

www.lifehacker.com
Ingenious methods for doing everything from setting a table to boiling an egg faster and smarter.

www.napo.net
The website of the National Association of Professional Organizers. A good resource if you need to hire an extra pair of hands to encourage de-cluttering—of the physical or mental variety.

www.noregretsparenting.com
This is the website of a pediatrician and hands-on dad, who encourages us to find the time for our children and teaches smart ways to make that time even more special (he had me at pajama walk!).

www.peterwalshdesign.com
This website is full of really clear de-cluttering and organizing tips, and Peter just oozes encouragement, so it's a great place for inspiring yourself to tackle that scary junk drawer.

www.scarymommy.com
Jill Smokler is an author and mom whose latest blog entries will make you laugh out loud and give you your full day's quota of mom-to-mom empathy.

www.sobeorganized.com
My website and blog, where I discuss time and space management and the tips and philosophies I use to make my own life less frazzled and more focused.

www.ted.com
A great way to spend twenty minutes—hearing your favorite author or someone you've never heard of share nuggets from their book or their lifetime of research. The talks run the gamut from inspirational to highly technical. Each talk is guaranteed to teach you something new.

ACKNOWLEDGMENTS

WRITING this book has been both an honor and a time management challenge of its own, as I juggled the book's "needs" along with the needs of my family. Thank you to the many people who encouraged and supported me along the way.

To Mum and Dad: Thank you for always allowing me to follow my "next great idea," however adventurous and crazy some of them have been. I hope I have made you proud along the way.

To my brother, David: Thanks for coming along for the ride and allowing me to call you at ridiculous times to ask even more ridiculous questions. Caryn, thanks again for marrying David, and for the lovely Jack and Kayla.

To Ima Dina and Zaidy: Thanks for so graciously adopting me as one of your own. I respect you both a lot more than I let on.

To my Caroline-Niknam siblings-in-law: You have survived twenty years with me in the family, and thankfully, I don't think I ended up diluting the Caroline gene pool too much after all. You are each very special to me. I value our relationships, and I always appreciate you schlepping down to Miami.

Reuven, Soheila, and Omid, your kindness and sincerity makes our family even more special.

Leah, your breathtakingly incredible artwork (www.leahcaroline.com) inspires me constantly.

Civ, my beautiful sister-in-law, thank you for always being there through thick and thin—and more importantly thank you for being *you*.

Dr. Rachel, Dr. Malka, and Dr. Jennie, you guys are great. Keep making the world a healthier place, one body part at a time!

Daniel, thank you for being such an amazing uncle and for always being there for us.

Ari, thanks for the strategic guidance and fancy algorithms, but thanks even more for thinking I might understand those tables. Not a chance!

David, your legal smarts and mediation skills have helped this project (a.k.a. me) tremendously.

Rafi, you are a great guy and the best-dressed Caroline. I will stop there.

And, of course, my incredible "niblings" (Caroline terminology for the plural of nieces and nephews): Rafael, Menucha, Brocha, Simcha, Levi, Elana, Yosef, Binyomin, Ita, Esther, Shira, Yaakov, Jack, Lea, Abe, and Benson.

A special mention to the extended Finkelstein family—our shared motto of "family first" is incredibly touching. I'd also like to give a double special mention to Dr. Harley Rotbart for adopting my book as if it were his own, and to Jesse Stein for his advice and help.

My pumpkin-latte-flavored thanks go out to Amy, my editor turned book midwife. Thanks for prioritizing to bring Sophie and Rory to our Hebrew School. You came into my world at just the perfect time and I loved our meetings, where we essentially turned my frazzled thoughts into focused writing. And while I know you love your move up north, our desk at Starbucks lacks its luster without you.

Liana, your illustrations helped this book develop a personality of its own, and for that I thank you (and you are a lovely cousin). To the early readers and critics of the book, thank you for your honest feedback and constructive suggestions: Chani Baram, Ilise Binhak, Dr. Arlene Cardozo, Jamie Frank, Kathie Klarreich, Ali Larson, Bassy Mendelsohn, Abby Messer, Karen Miller, Rebecca Pfeiffer, Lisa Walker, and Rabbi Menachem Schmidt.

As the book took on a momentum of its own, the following people helped guide it into the world and onto the Web: Stephen Binhak,

David Caroline, Rick Bartow, and Carolyn Koslyn. Thank you to all of you. And special thanks to Hobbs Allison, Bryan Carroll, Corrin Foster, Angela Alwin, Kim Lance, and Aaron Hierholzer at Greenleaf Book Group for making the book a reality.

To my cheerleading squad, thank you for the trust and the faith you have in me: Gramma (a.k.a. Helen Finck), Chaya Sara Dalfin, Nava Borisute, Miriam Budchenevsky, Malka Cohen, Whitney Corderi, Rachel Creeger, Lisa Darsa, June Feith, Lucy Furman, Susan Godfrey, Gigi Grassinower, Rosa Johnson, Scott Johnson, Valerie Marchant, Cheryl Morris, Juliet Pope, Jeanie Schottenstein, Roberta Shapiro, Theodosia Southern, Libby Spalter, Miriam Spero, Jill Spero, Harriet Stein, Carol Weingrod, Evelyn Wells, Brooke Yubero, Sara Rivka Zirkind, Yaakov's dream team headed up by the one and only Stacey, and the wonderful Dr. Maddy Mas.

I am especially thankful to Bluma Gittel Whitt (best virtual assistant ever), Nomi Yerushalmy, Dina Levertov, and Chava Schmidt for being available to me 24/6. And to our beloved babysitters past and present, Isa, Jacqui, and Andrea.

To the super-friendly Starbucks baristas at my three satellite "offices" in Key Biscayne, Sky Lake, and Hollywood. This book could not have been written without your copious quantities of lovingly brewed caffeine.

To my fellow Key Biscayne Jewish community residents and snowbirds, thanks for making our island a haven for spirituality and for the ways in which you enrich our lives personally.

To my fellow Chabad rabbis' wives around the globe: I salute you all for the incredible work you do and the lives you touch. And of course to the Rebbe, Rabbi Schneerson, whose unwavering belief in the inherent goodness within everyone serves as such an inspiration to me personally.

Seeing as I repeatedly confess publicly that I steer clear of doing things perfectly, I am quite sure that I have managed to leave some important people out, and for that I sincerely apologize.

Finally, *achron achron chaviv* ("we save the best for last"), to my children, Avremel, Menachem, Yossi, Sara, Yaakov, Chana, and Rosa, for creating the chaos that needed to be systemized, and for filling my life with unimaginable joy and challenging me to be a better person along the way. And, mostly, to my husband, Yoel, thank you for all that you do on a daily basis to make me feel supported and loved, even when I am frazzled and unfocused. For those reasons, and a few other more personal ones, I am honored to be your wife.

They say it isn't so much what an author writes, but what they whisper. I hope this book whispers hope and encouragement to you. No matter how frazzled your life has become, there is a way to live a calmer, more focused life for each of us. And so, with a humble nod of my head to Hashem, G-d almighty, for all the blessings He has given me, I present this book to you.

ABOUT THE AUTHORS

Rivka Caroline

RIVKA is a mom, rabbi's wife, and professional time management consultant in the Miami, Florida, area. She holds a bachelor's degree in psychology and will be completing her master's in psychology in 2013. She teaches individuals, small businesses, and teams within corporations how to leverage their time to work effectively and find time for the things that count. Perhaps more important, Rivka has seven children and is still quite relaxed and sane and able to find time for what matters. People often ask her how she "does it all." This book is her detailed response. (Spoiler alert: She *doesn't* actually do it all!)

Amy Sweeting

AMY is a freelance editor and writer based in Amherst, Massachusetts. She has authored, ghostwritten, and edited several books and publications for a diverse range of clients and organizations. Amy has only two children (though sometimes they seem like seven), but still has a fair amount of chaos in her life. After fifteen years of resisting her husband's suggestion to plan out the family's meals for the week, she finally gave it a try (at Rivka's prodding) and is amazed at how it has made evenings so much more relaxed. Her husband is very sweetly resisting the urge to say "I told you so."

CONTACT
RIVKA CAROLINE

- For speaking availability or speaking schedule
- To order 20 or more copies of the book
- To schedule a personal time management coaching appointment, whether in person or by phone

Please visit us at sobeorganized.com